Anti Inflammatory Cookbook

LEARN HOW TO REDUCE INFLAMMATION AND STAY HEALTHY WITH 50 EASY ANTI INFLAMMATORY RECIPES AND A 4-WEEK PLAN

Martin Cameron

Table of Contents

Introduction 1

Part 1: The Anti-Inflammatory Diet Explained.. 2

Chapter 1: Symptoms - Risks & Foods to Avoid... 3

    How to Eliminate Risks.. 4
    How to Treat Inflammation 4
    What to Avoid Using an Anti-Inflammatory Diet Plan................................ 5

Chapter 2: The Anti-Inflammatory Kitchen - Food to Eat 8

    Dairy Products 8
    Protein Options 8
    Whole Grains 9
    Vegetables 10
    Fruits 11
    Spices 12

Part 2: Anti-Inflammatory Recipes.. 13

Chapter 3: Breakfast Favorites 14

    Avocado Egg Boats - Air Fryer... 14
    Bacon & Egg Breakfast Muffins.. 15
    Baked Eggs In An Avocado... 16
    Breakfast Skillet 17
    Cocoa-Chia Pudding with Raspberries... 18
    Egg White Scramble with Cherry Tomatoes & Spinach......................... 20
    Eggs with Brussel Sprouts.. 21
    Huevos Rancheros... 22
    Kale & Goat Cheese Frittata Cups.. 23
    Mackerel & Eggs.. 24
    Mixed Vegetable Patties - Instant Pot... 25

    Quinoa Pancakes 26

    Scrambled Eggs 27

Cereal Options 28

    Barley Porridge 28

    Blueberry Hemp Seed Breakfast Oatmeal 29

    Coconut & Walnut Porridge 30

    Easy Quinoa 31

    Flaxseed Porridge 32

    Oats & Cherries 33

    Pineapple Oatmeal 34

Smoothies 35

    Cantaloupe Smoothies 35

    Cherry Coconut Smoothies 36

    Fresh Fruit Smoothie 37

    Ginger Carrot & Turmeric Smoothie 38

    Green Smoothies 40

    High-Protein Strawberry Smoothie 41

    Latte Pumpkin Spice Smoothie 42

    Melon Green Tea Smoothie 43

    Spinach & Avocado Smoothie 44

Other Beverages 45

    Healthy Turmeric Milk 45

    Japanese Iced Matcha - Vegan 46

    Turmeric Ginger C-Boost Life Juice 47

Chapter 4: Lunch & Dinner Salad & Vegetable Favorites 48

Salads 48

    Brown Rice Salad 48

    Cantaloupe Salad 50

    Chicken Salad with Pineapple 51

    Chickpea Salad 52

    Cod Salad 53

    Combo Bean Salad 54

    Fennel - Citrus & Avocado Salad 55

Feta Tomato Salad 57
Healthy Detox Salad with Lemon-Parsley Dressing 58
Vinaigrette Vegetable Salad 60

Veggie Meal Dishes 61

Mediterranean Quinoa & Chickpea Bowl 61
Roasted Chickpea & Sweet Potato Pitas 63
Roasted Garlic Squash with Sun-Dried Tomatoes 65
Sweet Potato & Black Bean Rice Bowls 66

Chapter 5: Lunch & Dinnertime Soup Favorites 68

Anti-Inflammatory Green Soup 68
Asparagus - Creamy-Style Soup 69
Broccoli Soup 70
Cabbage Soup 71
Cauliflower Beef Curry 73
Chicken & Sweet Potato Soup 74
Curried-Style Fish Stew 75
Greek Lentil Soup 76
Healthy Egg Drop Soup 77
Minty Avocado Chilled Soup 78
Turmeric Chicken Soup 79
White Bean & Chicken Soup 80

Chapter 6: Poultry Favorites 81

Chicken Options 81

Balsamic Grilled Chicken Breast 81
Bruschetta Chicken - Instant Pot 82
Chicken with Green Beans 83
Chicken With Yogurt & Mango Sauce 84
Greek Chicken 85
Kung Pao Chicken 86
One-Pan Chicken Thighs 88
Rotisserie Chicken & Cabbage Shreds 89
Southern Fried Chicken 90
Teriyaki - Slow-Cooked 91

Turkey Options 92
    Black Olive & Feta Turkey Burgers.. 92
    Ground Turkey Bowls with Mushrooms & Cabbage Rice 93
    Mediterranean Turkey Skillet... 95
    Zucchini & Ground Turkey Skillet 96

Chapter 7: Pork & Lamb Favorites 97

    Cilantro-Lime Pork - Slow-Cooked 97
    Country-Style Slow-Cooked Ribs 98
    Garlic Pepper Pork with Warm Garbanzo Salad 100
    Pork & Cherry Tomatoes... 102
    Pork Tenderloin with Apple-Thyme Sweet Potatoes 103
    Quick Mu Shu Pork.. 105
    Sauerkraut & Pork Shoulder Roast- Slow-Cooked...........................106
    Shredded Pork Roast for Sandwiches... 107
    Tender Baby Back Ribs 109

Lamb Favorites 110
    Garlic-Thyme Lamb Chops 110
    Lamb with Minty Green Beans - Slow Cooked 111
    Quick & Easy Lamb Chops 112
    Saucy Lamb & Asparagus 113

Chapter 8: Seafood Favorites 114

    Broiled Sea Bass 114
    Creamy Salmon Pasta... 115
    Crispy Skillet Salmon with Lemon-Caper Dill Sauce 116
    Frozen Italian Fish - Instant Pot.. 117
    Garlic Roasted Salmon & Brussels Sprouts...................................... 118
    Greek Roasted Fish & Veggies 119
    Lemon Baked Cod 121
    Lemon Garlic Shrimp With Zucchini Pasta 122
    One-Pan Salmon & Mixed Vegetables Specialty 123
    Shrimp Scampi 125
    Tuna in Cucumber Cups... 126
    Tuna Salad With Olives & White Beans - Nicoise-Style 127

Chapter 9: Side Dishes - Sauces - Dressings & Condiments 129

Side Dishes 129
- Acorn Squash With Apples 129
- Baby Spinach Bites 130
- Baked Zucchini-Feta Noodles 131
- Brown Rice Pilaf 132
- Celery Root 133
- Creamy Coconut Rice 134
- Ginger-Marinated Grilled Portobello Mushrooms 136
- Grilled Eggplant & Tomato Pasta 137
- Pickled Baby Carrots 138
- Shallots & Brussels Sprouts 139

Sauces 140
- Basil Tomato Sauce 140
- BBQ Sauce 141
- Greek Yogurt Mayonnaise 142
- Roasted Red Pepper Sauce - Vegetarian 143

Dips 144
- Homemade Hummus 144
- Mango Salsa 145
- White Bean Dip 146

Dressings 147
- Asian Salad Dressing - Vegan-Friendly 147
- Creamy Salad Dressing or Sauce 148
- Turmeric Salad Dressing 149

Chapter 10: Snack Options 150
- Chicken Filled Lettuce Wrap 150
- Chicken Kabobs With Lemon Wedges 151
- Lentil Avocado Tacos 152
- Shrimp Kebabs 153

Finger Snacks 154
- Roasted Almonds 154

  Roasted Pumpkin Seeds 155
  Roasted Radish Chips 156
  Slow-Roasted Cashews 157
 Crackers 158
  Almond Crackers 158
  Baked Zucchini Chips 159
  Goat Cheese Crackers 160

Chapter 11: Dessert Options 161

 Almond-Cinnamon Meringues 161
 Ambrosia With Coconut & Toasted Almonds 162
 Applesauce 163
 Apricot-Turmeric & Lemon Sugar-Free Bars 164
 Baked Goat Cheese With Roasted Pistachios & Blackberries 166
 Berry Watermelon Pops 167
 Black Bean Brownies - Vegan-Friendly 168
 Blueberry Crisp 169
 Chickpea Brownies 171
 Chilled Kiwi Bars 172
 Chocolate-Covered Strawberries 173
 Chocolate-Dipped Frozen Bananas 174
 Chocolate Ganache Macarons 175
 Cinnamon Custard 176
 Coconut Chia Seed & Sweet Potato Pudding 178
 Coconut Figs 179
 Dark Chocolate Cherry Granola Bars 180
 Fruity Rice Pudding 182
 Ginger Spice Cookies 183
 Healthy Green Pudding 185
 Lemon-Blueberry Cheesecake Bars 186
 Lemon Sorbet - Ice Cream Maker 188
 Mocha Chocolate Cake - Keto-Friendly 189

Part 3: Four-Week Meal Plan 191

Chapter 12: Week 1 Anti Inflammatory Menu 192

Chapter 13: Week 2 Anti Inflammatory Menu 194

Chapter 14: Week 3 Anti Inflammatory Menu 196

Chapter 15: Week 4 Anti Inflammatory Menu 198

Conclusion 200

Other Books By This Author 203

Introduction

Congratulations on purchasing *Anti Inflammatory Cookbook,* and thank you for doing so.

Inflammation is composed of many symptoms - including heat, swelling, pain, heat, and redness of an affected organ or tissue. It's a natural way the body's immune system method or natural response to attack, injury, or infection.

Many of the recipes will provide you with meal prep suggestions for your convenience. It will be a tremendous aid to keep your diet under control. An anti-inflammatory diet favors vegetables, fruits, whole grains, foods containing omega-3 fatty acids, lean protein, spices, and healthy fats. It limits or discourages consuming red meats and processed foods, and red meats. The anti-inflammatory diet is not a specific regimen - but rather a style of eating.

Thanks again for choosing this book; make sure to leave a short review on Amazon if you enjoy it; I'd love to hear your thoughts!

# Part 1: The Anti-Inflammatory Diet Explained

Chapter 1:
Symptoms - Risks & Foods to Avoid

Depression, anxiety, stress, or sadness can impact your physical well-being. These emotions trigger chemical reactions in your body, leading to inflammation and a weakened immune system. Indication markers for inflammation can be any of the following:

- A joint that doesn't work properly
- Swollen joint - warm to the touch
- Painful or stiff joints
- Redness

You may also have other evident signs - including:

- Appetite loss
- Headaches
- Chills
- Fever
- Fatigue or loss of energy
- Muscle stiffness

How to Eliminate Risks

The best way to eliminate the risk is to seek professional help. Your physician will document your medical history and perform a physical exam to focus on the pattern of the joint pain, asking questions including whether you're stiffer in the morning and other symptoms. You will probably be asked to have several tests.

They'll also look at the results of X-rays and blood tests for biomarkers such as:

- Erythrocyte sedimentation rate (ESR)
- C-reactive protein (CRP)

How to Treat Inflammation

Take several steps to improve inflammation, including exercise, rest, medications, and possibly surgery to correct joint damage. Your treatment plan will depend on several things, including your type of disease, the medications you're taking, your age, your general health, and the severity of your symptoms.

The goals of treatment are to:

- You may begin to use physical therapy to improve muscle strength and joint movement.
- Eliminate activities that may aggravate pain.
- Slow down or control the disease process
- Lower your pain threshold through anti-inflammatory drugs or similar pain medications.
- Grab a cane to help eliminate some of the joint stress as needed.

What to Avoid Using an Anti-Inflammatory Diet Plan

Dairy

A 2017 review (52 clinical studies) concluded that dairy generally has anti-inflammatory effects, except for those allergic to cow's milk.

Whole Milk, Butter, & Cheese: Saturated fat is once again a plaguing issue. Opt for low-fat dairy products which do not have inflammation markers.

Vegetable Oils Galore

Margarine, shortening, baked goods including pancake mix, pies, cakes & cake mixes, frosting, doughnuts, ice cream, fried foods, fast food, or restaurant prepared food products, including ground beef, crackers, jerky sticks, potato or tortilla chips. Add non-dairy creamers, breakfast sandwiches, biscuits, frozen dinners or meat products, frozen pizzas, and so many more.

Instead, opt for these oils; vegetable, corn, soybean, sunflower, safflower, cottonseed, canola/rapeseed, peanut, or grapeseed oil.

Processed Foods

Soda - Cookies - Cakes - Sweets & Most Factory-Packaged Items: Sugar can cause your body to release inflammatory triggers called "cytokines." These are culprits that are easy to overeat - yet are not dense in nutrients. They can blaze the path to inflammation and create high cholesterol, high blood sugar, and weight gain.

Conventionally-raised (non-pasture-raised or non-grass-fed) chicken, beef, lamb, and pork are at the top of the list. Processed and high-fat red meat - such as hot dogs - exudes large amounts of saturated fat - if consumed daily - even in small amounts - can trigger inflammation. You also need to consider - sausage, bacon, bologna, deli meat, or jerky. Any meat products that do not deem the phrase "pasture-raised" or "grass-fed" on the package have been conventionally raised on corn or soy - grain-based diet!

Gluten

You will find gluten is an extremely common protein found in many foods we eat, including barley, wheat, and rye. You find it in many processed or baked foods, breakfast cereal, pasta, and bread - just about anywhere! Gluten provides no essential nutrients; it also doesn't contain anything harmful to the average person. However, it must be avoided by individuals who have celiac disease.

Refined Sugar

You will be looking for these types of sugar; cane, corn syrup, maltodextrin, brown rice syrup, galactose, disaccharides, evaporated cane syrup, or dextrose.

Refined sugars hide in soda, coffee/tea drinks, fruit juices, energy drinks, granola and protein bars, snack bars, cookies, candy, cereals, instant oatmeal packets, baked goods, bread, ice cream, flavored yogurts, canned soups, frozen dinners, condiments, pasta, salad dressings, and all kinds of sauces - bbq, pasta, etc.

Synthetic Sweeteners

These sweeteners can disrupt the ability of your body to metabolize glucose correctly and worsen inflammation. They can reduce the levels of good bacteria, which help with releasing your anti-inflammatory compounds. You will want to dodge saccharin, aspartame in Equal or Nutrasweet, sucralose as in Splenda, or saccharin such as found in Sweet N' Low.

Artificial Additives

Processed foods, no-calorie "diet" drinks, no-sugar-added foods, protein bars & powders, ice cream, candy, chewing gum, cereals, or almost 'any packaged food' will contain some form of artificial additive! Be careful as you shop and read those labels.

Chapter 2:
The Anti-Inflammatory Kitchen - Food to Eat

Dairy Products

Feta cheese contains friendly bacteria with anti-inflammatory effects that also promote intestinal and immune health. The feta is mostly made from sheep's milk.

Goat cheese is known for its creamy, distinct flavor with acid that has been shown to possess antibacterial and anti-inflammatory properties.

Yogurt protein and probiotics have anti-inflammatory roles. Recent studies have shown that daily yogurt consumption has been shown to prevent gut microbiota alteration, a common consequence of chronic opioid use.

Heavy cream in many of its recipes. If you do not have heavy cream, here is a simple fix for one cup:

- Mix whole milk (.66 or 2/3 cup)
- With melted butter (.33 or 1/3 cup)

Eggs with their vitamin D present will modulate the inflammatory response in rheumatoid arthritis. As a result, eggs are one of the best anti-inflammatory foods.

Protein Options

Fatty fish are an excellent source of protein and the long-chain omega-3 fatty acids DHA and EPA. These are a few of the examples:

- Mackerel
- Herring
- Salmon
- Tuna
- Shrimp
- Clams
- Sardines
- Trout
- Anchovies

Other Protein Options:

- Tofu
- Grass-fed steak
- Grass-fed hamburger
- Meat sauce made from grass-fed beef
- Lean pork

Whole Grains

Unrefined grains, including oatmeal, brown rice, and whole-wheat bread, and others tend to maintain higher fiber counts, which also helps lower inflammation. Whole grains contain several anti-inflammatory compounds, including B vitamins and protein.

Homemade Healthy Breadcrumbs
Here is a quick way to prepare fresh and healthy breadcrumbs:

1. You will make 1/3 cup or 1/2 cup of dry crumbs from one bread slice.
2. Choose whole-wheat bread and trim away the crusts.
3. Slice the bread and toss it into a food processor to create coarse breadcrumbs as desired.
4. If you prefer a batch of dried crumbs, set the oven to 250° Fahrenheit/121° Celsius.
5. Toss the coarse/fine breadcrumbs onto a baking tray and bake them for 10 to 15 minutes.

Vegetables

These are just a few of the veggies that are excellent for an anti=inflammatory diet:

Tomatoes are high in vitamin C, potassium, and lycopene.

Bell peppers and chili peppers are also loaded with antioxidants and vitamin c.

Broccoli is rich in sulforaphane, an antioxidant that fights inflammation by reducing cytokine levels that motivate inflammation.

Mushrooms including truffles, portobello, and shiitake. They're extremely low in calories and rich in copper, selenium, and B vitamins.

Beans provide an abundance of fiber, shown to reduce inflammation and help lower cholesterol.

Seeds - *Nuts & Legumes:* Healthy veggies will provide you with additional fiber, protein, magnesium, phytochemicals, and protein to your body. Some may have higher calorie counts. Consider some of these options:

- Kidney beans - 215 calories per one cup - 256 grams
- Peas - 125 calories per one cup - 160 grams
- Pistachios - 170 calories per .5 cup
- Almonds - 622 calories per 100 grams
- Cashews - 585 calories per 100 grams
- Peanuts - 427 calories per 73 grams or for each .5 cup

Raw walnuts, unsalted nuts, and seeds, such as the omega-3-rich walnut, for an anti-inflammatory snack have proven to help reduce LDL cholesterol, blood pressure and improve brain health.

Fruits

Berries are loaded with vitamins, minerals, and fiber. These are the most common:

- Blueberries
- Strawberries
- Blackberries
- Raspberries

Avocado. Avocado leads the path with vitamin E and monounsaturated fats, two anti-inflammatory powerhouses that help improve skin, joints, brain function, and cardiovascular health.

Grapes contain anthocyanins to help lower inflammation.

They might also decrease the risk of diabetes, heart disease, obesity, Alzheimer's, and eye disorders.

Cherries are delicious and rich in antioxidants, such as anthocyanins and catechins, which fight inflammation.

Dried figs are a good source of two types of phytochemicals, polyphenols, and flavonoids, which work to ease existing inflammation and prevent free radicals from triggering new inflammation.

Extra-virgin olive oil is one of the healthiest fats you can eat. It's rich in monounsaturated fats, which provide numerous health benefits. Studies link the oil to a reduced risk of serious conditions such as heart disease.

Green tea contains antioxidants and anti-inflammatory properties to help lower your risk of conditions for ailments, including heart disease, Alzheimer's disease, cancer, obesity, and other conditions.

Spices

Homemade Italian Seasoning
Combine the following dried fixings to make three tablespoons of Italian seasoning:

- Oregano (1 tbsp.)
- Basil (2 tsp.)
- Sage (1 tsp.)
- Thyme - not ground (2 tsp.)
- Rosemary (.5 tsp.)

Turmeric is a spice that conveys an earthy, strong flavor often used in curries and other Indian dishes. It contains curcumin, a powerful anti-inflammatory nutrient that helps to lower/reduce inflammation related to arthritis and other diseases.

Dark Chocolate & Cocoa is a rich and delicious option loaded with antioxidants to help reduce inflammation.

Part 2:
Anti-Inflammatory Recipes

Chapter 3: Breakfast Favorites

Avocado Egg Boats - Air Fryer

Servings: 2
Total Required Time: 16-18 minutes

Essential Ingredients:
- Avocado (1)
- Eggs (2 large)
  To Taste:
- Fresh parsley & chives
- Salt & pepper

Method of Prep:
1. Chop the parsley and chives. Heat the Air Fryer unit to reach 350° Fahrenheit/177° Celsius.
2. Remove the pit from the avocado. Slice and scoop out part of the flesh. Shake with the seasonings.
3. Add an egg to each half and place it into the basket. Air-fry for six minutes.
4. Serve with some additional parsley and chives if desired.

Bacon & Egg Breakfast Muffins

Servings: 12
Total Required Time: 35 minutes

Essential Ingredients:
- Eggs (8 large)
- Turkey bacon (8 slices)
- Green onion (.66 or 2/3 cup)

Method of Prep:
1. Warm the oven to reach 350° Fahrenheit/177° Celsius.
2. Spritz the muffin tin wells using a cooking oil spray. Chop the onions and set them aside for now.
3. Prepare a large skillet using the medium temperature setting. Fry the bacon until it's crispy and arrange it on a layer of paper towels to drain the fat. Chop it into small pieces after it has cooled.
4. Whisk the eggs, bacon, and green onions, mixing well until the fixings are incorporated.
5. Dump the egg mixture into the muffin tin (halfway full).
6. Bake it for about 20 to 25 minutes. Cool slightly to serve.
7. Note: Some may not be able to tolerate the bacon. Choose another lean meat instead.

Baked Eggs In An Avocado

Servings: 1
Total Required Time: 25 minutes

Essential Ingredients:
- Avocado (half of 1)
- Olive oil (1 tbsp.)
- Egg (1)
- Cheddar shredded cheese (.5 cup)

Method of Prep:
1. Warm the oven to 425° Fahrenheit/218° Celsius.
2. Discard the avocado pit and remove just enough of the 'insides' to add the egg. Drizzle using oil - break the egg into the shell.
3. Top it off using the cheese. Pop it into the oven to bake until the egg is the way you prefer (15 min.). Serve as desired.

Breakfast Skillet

Servings: 2
Total Required Time: 10 minutes

Essential Ingredients:
- Organic ground turkey/grass-fed beef (.75 to 1 lb./340-450 g)
- Organic eggs (6)
- Salsa - your preference (1 cup)

Method of Prep:
1. Warm the skillet and add oil (medium-temperature setting).
2. When heated, add the turkey and simmer until the pink is gone.
3. Fold in the salsa and simmer for two to three minutes.
4. Crack the eggs over the turkey base. Put a top on the pan and cook for seven minutes until the egg whites are opaque.

Cocoa-Chia Pudding with Raspberries

Servings: 1
Total Required Time: 8 hours or up to three days (set time)

Essential Ingredients:
- Almond milk/another preferred choice - unsweetened (.5 cup)
- Cocoa powder - unsweetened (.5 tsp.)
- Chia seeds (2 tbsp.)
- Pure maple syrup (2 tsp.)
- Vanilla extract (.25 tsp.)
- Toasted sliced almonds - divided (1 tbsp.)
- Fresh raspberries, divided (.5 cup)

Method of Prep:
1. Combine the chosen milk with the syrup, chia, cocoa, and vanilla in a mixing container with a lid.
2. Close it and pop it into the fridge (8 hr. minimum) for up to three days.

3. At serving time, scoop half of the pudding into a serving dish, add half of the almonds and berries, and the remainder of the pudding.
4. Garnish the dish using the rest of the raspberries and almonds.

Egg White Scramble with Cherry Tomatoes & Spinach

Servings: 4
Total Required Time: 10 minutes

Essential Ingredients:
- Olive oil (1 tbsp.)
- Eggs (1 whole + 10 egg whites)
- Salt (.5 tsp.)
- Black pepper (.25 tsp.)
- Garlic (1 clove)
- Fresh baby spinach - tightly packed (2 cups)
- Halved cherry tomatoes (2 cups)
- Half & Half - see recipe chap. 2 (.5 cup)
- Finely grated parmesan cheese (.25 cup)

Method of Prep:
1. Whisk the eggs, pepper, salt, and milk.
2. Prepare a skillet using the med-hi heat setting.
3. Mince and toss in the garlic when the pan is hot. Sauté them for ½ minute.
4. Pour in the tomatoes and spinach. Sauté them for one minute. The tomatoes should be softened, and the spinach wilted.
5. Add the egg mixture into the pan using the medium-temperature setting. Fold the egg gently as it cooks (2-3 min.).
6. Transfer the pan to a cool burner, and sprinkle with a sprinkle of cheese before serving.

Eggs with Brussel Sprouts

Servings: 2
Total Required Time: 20 minutes

Essential Ingredients:
- Black pepper & salt (.5 tsp. of each)
- Butter/olive oil (2 tbsp.)
- Eggs (2)
- Brussel sprouts - freshly grated (2 cups)

Method of Prep:
1. Grate and fry the sprouts in the oil/butter for nine to ten minutes until they are slightly soft and just beginning to brown.
2. Make two shallow holes in the cooked sprouts with the back of a spoon and break one of the eggs into each hole.
3. Cook for five more minutes without stirring while the eggs cook. Sprinkle on the pepper and the salt as desired and serve.

Huevos Rancheros

Servings: 1
Total Required Time: 15 minutes

Essential Ingredients:
- Cilantro - fresh (1 tbsp.)
- Avocado (half of 1)
- Black pepper (1 tsp.)
- Eggs (2)
- Garlic (2 cloves)
- Jalapeno (1)
- Olive oil (2 tbsp.)
- Orange bell pepper (half of 1)
- Salt (.5 tsp.)
- Tomato (1)
- Yellow onion (half of 1)

Method of Prep:
1. Mince/chop and sauté the garlic, onion, bell pepper, and jalapeno in half of the olive oil for five minutes, mixing well.
2. Pour in the diced tomatoes and fry this for an additional five minutes.
3. While the mix is frying, whisk the eggs in a small mixing container - dump them over the veggie mix in the skillet, often stirring until the eggs are scrambled to the consistency you prefer.
4. Serve with slices of fresh avocado.

Kale & Goat Cheese Frittata Cups

Servings: 6-8
Total Required Time: 35-40 minutes

Essential Ingredients:
- Olive oil (3 tbsp.)
- Lacinato kale (2 cups - chopped)
- Garlic (1 clove)
- Red pepper flakes (.25 tsp.)
- Eggs (8 large)
- Salt (.25 tsp.)
- Black pepper (1 dash)
- Dried thyme (.5 tsp.)
- Goat cheese - crumbled (.25 cup)
- Suggested: 10-inch nonstick skillet & 8-cup muffin tin

Method of Prep:
1. Set the oven to reach 350° Fahrenheit/177° Celsius.
2. Discard the kale ribs - thoroughly rinse and dry the leaves.
3. You want two cups of trimmed kale, sliced into ½-inch wide strips.
4. Prepare the skillet using a med-high temperature setting - add oil (1 tbsp.).
5. Thinly slice and sauté the garlic for 30 seconds. Toss in the kale and red pepper flakes - sautéing till wilted (1-2 min.).
6. Whisk the eggs with salt and pepper in a mixing container - add the kale and thyme.
7. Lightly grease the muffin cups using the rest of the oil (2 tbsp.); you may also use butter or nonstick spray.
8. Sprinkle the tops with the cheese. Bake till they're set in the center (25-30 min.).
9. Enjoy it piping hot, but leftovers can be refrigerated and reheated for up to a week.

Mackerel & Eggs

Servings: 2-3
Total Required Time: 10 minutes

Essential Ingredients:
- Eggs (4)
- Butter/oil of choice - for frying (2 tbsp.)
- Canned mackerel in tomato sauce (8 oz. or 230 g)
- Lettuce (2 oz. or 56 g)
- Red onion (half of 1)
- Olive oil (.25 cup)
- Black pepper & salt (as desired)

Method of Prep:
1. Warm a skillet and prepare the eggs in the butter.
2. Add lettuce to a platter and layer with onion and mackerel.
3. Arrange the eggs to the side, seasoning as desired using pepper and salt.
4. Spritz the oil over the salad and serve.

Mixed Vegetable Patties - Instant Pot

Servings: 1
Total Required Time: 20 minutes

Essential Ingredients:
- Cauliflower florets (1 cup)
- Frozen mixed vegetables (1 bag)
- Water (1.5 cups)
- Flax meal (1 cup)
- Olive oil (2 tbsp.)

Method of Prep:
1. Fill the Instant Pot with the water and add the veggies to the steamer basket. Secure the lid and set the timer for four to five minutes using the high-pressure setting.
2. Quick-release the pressure and drain.
3. Use a potato masher and stir in the flax meal. Shape into four patties.
4. Select the sauté function in a clean pot and pour in the oil.
5. Prepare the patties until they are golden brown or for about three minutes per side before serving.

Quinoa Pancakes

Servings: 8
Total Required Time: 10 minutes

Essential Ingredients:
- Coconut sugar (2 tbsp.)
- Quinoa flour (1.5 cups)
- Unsweetened applesauce (.5 cup)
- Lemon juice (1 tbsp.)
- Nonfat milk (.5 cup)
- Baking soda (1 tsp.)

Method of Prep:
1. Use the food processor to combine the sugar with the applesauce, milk, sugar, baking soda, lemon juice, and quinoa. Pulse well.
2. Heat a skillet using the medium-temperature setting.
3. Pour the pancake batter into the warm pan.
4. Cook them for three minutes per side. Continue until you finish all of the batter.
5. Divide between the plates and serve.

Scrambled Eggs

Servings: 2
Total Required Time: 10 minutes

Essential Ingredients:
- Eggs (4 large)
- Salt & pepper (as desired)
- Skim or 1% milk (.25 cup)
- Fresh parsley (2 tbsp.)

Method of Prep:
1. Finely chop the parsley. Break eggs into a bowl and add milk, pepper, salt, and parsley. Whisk until thoroughly combined.
2. Warm a skillet using the med-high temperature setting and lightly spritz it using the cooking spray.
3. Pour eggs into the pan, pushing them around the pan with a non-metal spatula until the eggs are set and no liquid remains (5 min.).
4. Scrape the pan and continue stirring to keep the eggs light and fluffy.
5. Note: For the best results, don't use egg beaters!

Cereal Options

Barley Porridge

Servings: 4
Total Required Time: 35 minutes

Essential Ingredients:
- Unsweetened almond milk - 2 cups + more for serving
- Water (2 cups)
- Barley (1 cup)
- Blueberries (.5 cup)
- Wheat berries (1 cup)
- Pomegranate seeds (.5 cup)
- Roasted and chopped hazelnuts (.5 cup)
- Raw honey (.25 cup)

Method of Prep:
1. Pour and heat the almond milk, water, wheat berries, and barley in a saucepan using the medium-high temperature setting.
2. Once boiling, adjust the temperature to the low setting. Simmer for 25 minutes.
3. Stir often. When done, top each serving with the pomegranate seeds, a tablespoon of honey, blueberries, and hazelnuts. Give it a splash of almond milk. Serve.

Blueberry Hemp Seed Breakfast Oatmeal

Servings: 2
Total Required Time: 10-12 minutes - varies

Essential Ingredients:
- Unsweetened almond milk/water (1 cup)
- Ground cinnamon (.5 tsp.)
- Hemp seed hearts (.5 cup)
- Flaxseed meal (.5 cup)
- Swerve (2 tbsp.)
- Unsweetened coconut flakes (1 tbsp.)
- Fresh blueberries (.25 cup)
- Vanilla extract (1 tsp.)
- Sliced almonds (1 tbsp.)

Method of Prep:
1. Place a saucepan over a med-high temperature setting using the stovetop. Pour in the milk, vanilla extract, and cinnamon. Stir.
2. Toss in the hemp seed hearts and flaxseed meal. Change the temperature on the stove to medium heat.
3. Stir in the sweetener. Keep the mixture on the heat (uncovered) until the oatmeal thickens.
4. Serve in a bowl and top with almonds, blueberries, and other keto-friendly toppings.

Coconut & Walnut Porridge

Servings: 1
Total Required Time: 10-12 minutes

Essential Ingredients:
- Almond butter (1 tbsp.)
- Coconut milk (.5 cup)
- Crushed walnuts (3 tbsp.)
- Desiccated coconut (1.5 tbsp.)
- Coconut oil (1 tbsp.)
- Cinnamon (.25 tsp.)

Method of Prep:
1. Warm the oil with the almond butter and milk in a small saucepan.
2. Once it's boiling, stir in the coconut and walnuts.
3. Mix well and transfer the pan to a cool burner.
4. Wait for about five minutes and serve.

Easy Quinoa

Servings: 6
Total Required Time: Under 30 minutes

Essential Ingredients:
- Water/broth (2 cups)
- Quinoa (1 cup)

Method of Prep:
1. Whisk and add the fixings in a saucepan. Wait for it to boil.
2. Cover with a top and adjust the temperature setting to low.
3. Simmer till the liquid is absorbed (15-20 min.). Fluff with a fork.
4. Have a delicious bowl in under ½ hour. Pop it in the fridge to enjoy for up to four days.

Flaxseed Porridge

Servings: 1
Total Required Time: 5-6 minutes

Essential Ingredients:
- Flaxseed - plain or roasted for nutty-like (3 tbsp.)
- Coconut milk - unsweetened (.5 cup)
- Butter (2.5 tsp.)
- Grapeseed oil (2 tsp.)
- Wild/frozen blueberries (2 tbsp.)
- Cinnamon (0.125 or 1/8 tsp.)

Method of Prep:
1. Whisk the milk with the flaxseed in a microwave-safe bowl. Use one that will hold at least two cups of liquid. Cook until the mixture starts rising (30-45 sec.).
2. Transfer the container to the countertop and wait for it to cool for one minute.
3. Mix in the butter, oil, blueberries, and cinnamon. Stir thoroughly to coat the blueberries. Don't over-stir; it will make the porridge gummy. *Note:* You can also make it using a small saucepan on the stovetop.
4. Once boiling, transfer the pan to a cool burner to serve.

Oats & Cherries

Servings: 6
Total Required Time: 20-25 minutes

Essential Ingredients:
- Cherries (2 cups)
- Oats - old-fashioned type (2 cups)
- Water (6 cups)
- Vanilla extract (1 tsp.)
- Almond milk (1 cup)
- Cinnamon (1 tsp.)

Method of Prep:
1. Remove the pits and slice the cherries.
2. Combine all of the fixings in a small saucepan.
3. Wait for it to boil using the medium-high heat setting.
4. Cook the mixture for 15 minutes and divide it into serving bowls.

Pineapple Oatmeal

Servings: 4
Total Required Time: 35 minutes

Essential Ingredients:
- Walnuts (1 cup)
- Pineapple (2 cups)
- Oats - old-fashioned (2 cups)
- Nonfat milk (2 cups)
- Ginger (1 tbsp.)
- Eggs (2)
- Stevia (2 tbsp.)
- Vanilla extract (2 tsp.)
- Also Needed: Ramekins (4)

Method of Prep:
1. Set the oven temperature at 400° Fahrenheit/204° Celsius.
2. Chop the nuts and pineapple. Grate the ginger.
3. Combine the oats with walnuts, pineapple, and ginger. Stir well and divide into the ramekins.
4. Whisk the eggs with milk, vanilla, and stevia. Empty the egg mixture over the oats.
5. Arrange the ramekins in the oven.
6. Bake for about 25 minutes. Serve when ready.

Smoothies

Cantaloupe Smoothies

Servings: 2
Total Required Time: 5 minutes

Essential Ingredients:
- Frozen cantaloupe (2.5 cups)
- Nonfat or low-fat milk (.5 cup)
- Frozen banana (1 sliced)
- Nonfat vanilla Greek yogurt (5.5 oz./160 g carton)
- Ice (.5 cup)
- Honey (1 tsp.)

Method of Prep:
1. Peel, cube, and freeze the cantaloupe.
2. Place the milk, banana, yogurt, ice, and honey in a blender.
3. Work and mix the fixings till incorporated and creamy.
4. Toss in the cantaloupe pieces - process until incorporated and creamy smooth.
5. Serve immediately.

Cherry Coconut Smoothies

Servings: 2
Total Required Time: 5-6 minutes

Essential Ingredients:
- Cherries (1 cup)
- Coconut water (.5 cup)
- Ice (1 cup)
- Almond milk (.5 cup)

Method of Prep:
1. Discard the cherry pits.
2. Measure and add the fixings into a blender - pulse till it's incorporated and smooth.

Fresh Fruit Smoothie

Servings: 4
Total Required Time: 12-15 minutes

Essential Ingredients:
- Fresh pineapple chunks (1 cup)
- Cantaloupe or other melon chunks (.5 cup)
- Fresh strawberries (1 cup)
- Juice (from 2 oranges)
- Water (1 cup - cold)
- Agave nectar/sub honey (1 tbsp.)

Method of Prep:
1. Discard the rind from the pineapple and melon - slice them into pieces.
2. Remove the stems from strawberries.
3. Toss each of the fixings into a blender. Mix them till they're incorporated and creamy smooth.
4. Serve the smoothies cold.

Ginger Carrot & Turmeric Smoothie

Servings: 2
Total Required Time: 10 minutes

Essential Ingredients:

The Juice:
- Carrots (2 cups)
- Filtered water (1.5 cups)

The Smoothie:
- Ripe banana (1 large + more for sweetness as desired)
- Frozen or fresh pineapple (1 cup or 140 g)
- Fresh ginger (.5 tbsp.)
- Carrot juice (.5 cup/120 ml.)
- Ground turmeric (.25 tsp.)
- Cinnamon (.5 tsp.)
- Lime juice (1 tbsp.)
- Unsweetened almond milk (1 cup or 240 ml.)
- Suggested: High-powered blender

Method of Prep:

1. Add the water and carrots to the blender. Mix till it's incorporated and smooth.

2. Add more water as needed, scraping down its sides. Keep the juice in the refrigerator.
3. Toss the rest of the fixings into the blender for the smoothie and mix thoroughly.
4. Serve in two chilled glasses.

Green Smoothies

Servings: 4 - 170 g/6 oz. portions
Total Required Time: 6 minutes

Essential Ingredients:
- Banana (1)
- Juice (1 lemon/about 4 tbsp.)
- Strawberries (.5 cup)
- Berries - such as blueberries or blackberries (.5 cup)
- Baby spinach (2 oz./approx. 2 cups)
- Fresh mint (as desired)
- Ice or cold water (1 cup)

Method of Prep:
1. Toss each of the fixings into a blender or juicer.
2. Puree and serve in chilled mugs.

High-Protein Strawberry Smoothie

Servings: 1
Total Required Time: 10 minutes

Essential Ingredients:
- Low-fat cottage cheese -low-salt (.5 cup)
- 1% milk (.75 cup)
- Fresh/frozen strawberries (1 cup)**

Method of Prep:
1. Toss each of the fixings into the mixing container dish (ex. Nutribullet cup).
2. Blend each of the fixings till creamy.
3. Pour it into a tall-chilled glass to serve.
4. Note** You can substitute the berries for a banana, sliced mango, or a half cup of another favorite berry.

Latte Pumpkin Spice Smoothie

Servings: 1
Total Required Time: 6 minutes

Essential Ingredients:
- Frozen vanilla yogurt (.33 cup)
- Pumpkin (.33 cup)
- Ground cinnamon (.5 tsp.)
- Instant coffee (1 tsp.)
- Pumpkin pie spice (.5 tsp.)
- Plain Greek yogurt (.25 cup)
- Pure maple syrup (1 tsp.)
- Almond milk - unsweetened (8 oz./230 g)

Method of Prep:
1. Empty all of the components into the cup of a high-speed mixer, such as a Nutri-Bullet.
2. Pour the milk into the cup up to the max fill line.
3. Pulse till it's consistent and smooth to serve.

Melon Green Tea Smoothie

Servings: 2
Total Required Time: 6-7 minutes

Essential Ingredients:
- Green tea (1 cup - brewed)
- Frozen pineapple chunks (1 cup)
- Pear (1 cored & cut into chunks)
- Cantaloupe chunks (1 cup)
- Greek yogurt - plain (.5 cup)
- Fresh mint (4 leaves + additional to taste)

Method of Prep:
1. Brew the tea and cool. Measure and combine the tea with the pineapple, cantaloupe, pear, yogurt, and mint leaves in a blender.
2. Mix till it's creamy smooth to serve in two cold glasses.

Spinach & Avocado Smoothie

Servings: 1
Total Required Time: 5-6 minutes

Essential Ingredients:
- Plain yogurt - nonfat (1 cup)
- Frozen banana (1)
- Avocado (¼ of 1)
- Fresh spinach (1 cup)
- Honey (1 tsp.)
- Water (2 tbsp.)

Method of Prep:
1. Toss the yogurt with avocado, honey, banana, water, and spinach in a blender.
2. Let the mixture work and puree till it's creamy smooth.
3. Serve in a chilled mug.

Other Beverages

Healthy Turmeric Milk

Servings: 1
Total Required Time: 12-15 minutes

Essential Ingredients:
- Fresh turmeric & ginger root (1.5-inch/4-cm piece each)
- Honey (1 tbsp.)
- Unsweetened almond milk (1 cup)
- Optional: Ground turmeric & ginger (1 pinch each)

Method of Prep:
1. Peel, grate and toss the turmeric and ginger root with the honey in a mixing container.
2. Warm the milk in a saucepan using a med-low temperature setting. Once small bubbles start forming around the edges, adjust the temperature to low.
3. Transfer about two tablespoons of milk to the turmeric mixture - allowing it to soften and melt into a paste-like mixture.
4. Mix the turmeric paste into milk in the saucepan. Adjust the temperature setting to med-low - simmer till the mix is thoroughly combined. Blend it using an immersion blender for a smooth texture.
5. Pour the turmeric tea into a mug and top with ground turmeric and cinnamon.
6. Enjoy your milk.

Japanese Iced Matcha - Vegan

Servings: 1
Total Required Time: 5 minutes

Essential Ingredients:
- Matcha powder (1-2 tsp./to taste)
- Ice (5-7 cubes)
- Water (cold - 1 to 1.5 cups - to top off)
- Sweetener options (see notes)
- For Iced Matcha: Milk - dairy-free - your preference (see notes)

Method of Prep:
1. Put the cubed ice into a container such as a sealable jar.
2. Add the matcha powder and water.
3. Vigorously shake till it's smooth to serve.
4. Notes: For an iced matcha latte, use equal parts cold water and dairy-free milk; shake till it's smooth, or fill the jar about halfway with water. Top it off with a cold-frothed plant-based milk such as almond, coconut, soy, or oat.
5. For a sweeter matcha, add one to two teaspoons of sweetener of choice (maple syrup, honey, or agave).

Turmeric Ginger C-Boost Life Juice

Servings: 1
Total Required Time: 5 minutes

Essential Ingredients:
- Fuji apples (2)
- Orange (1 sectioned)
- Lemon (half of 1)
- Fresh ginger (1-inch/3-cm piece)
- Ground turmeric (.5 tsp.)

Method of Prep:
1. Core and slice the apple - peel the orange and lemon.
2. Process orange, apples, ginger, and lemon, through a juicer - stir in turmeric until evenly incorporated. It misses the keto scale, but it is delicious.
3. Serve when ready.

Chapter 4:
Lunch & Dinner Salad & Vegetable Favorites

Salads

Brown Rice Salad

Servings: 6
Total Required Time: 60 minutes

Essential Ingredients:
- Uncooked brown rice (1.5 cups)
- Water (3 cups)
- Red bell pepper (1)
- Frozen green peas (1 cup)
- Raisins (.5 cup)
- Sweet onion - ex. Vidalia (¼ of 1)
- Kalamata olives (.25 cup)
- Dijon mustard (1.25 tsp.)
- Vegetable oil (.5 cup)
- Balsamic vinegar (.25 cup)
- Black pepper & salt (as desired)
- Feta cheese (.25 cup)

Method of Prep:
1. Prep the veggies. Thaw the peas. Thinly slice the pepper, and chop the onion and olives.
2. Prepare the rice and water using a high-temperature setting.
3. Once boiling, lower the setting to med-low and put a top on the pot. Simmer it for 45 to 50 minutes.
4. Whisk the mustard with vinegar and oil for the dressing.
5. Combine the olives, onion, raisins, peppers, and peas in a mixing bowl.

6. Mix it all with a portion of pepper and salt. Garnish it with feta and serve.

Cantaloupe Salad

Servings: 3
Total Required Time: 5-7 minutes

Essential Ingredients:
- Cantaloupe (1 cup)
- Diced cucumber (1)
- Lime juice (1 tsp.)
- Mint leaves (2 tsp.)

Method of Prep:
1. Combine the recipe components until thoroughly mixed.
2. Drizzle with the lime juice and serve.

Chicken Salad with Pineapple

Servings: 8
Total Required Time: 15 minutes

Essential Ingredients:
- Olive oil (1 tbsp.)
- Baby spinach leaves (4 cups)
- Red onions (.5 cup)
- Chicken breasts (4 @ 5 oz./140 g each)
- Broccoli florets (2 cups)
- Unsweetened pineapple chunks (8 oz./230 g can)

Method of Prep:
1. Discard the bones and the skin from the chicken and dice it into cubes.
2. Thinly slice the onions.
3. Warm the oil using a medium-temperature setting in a skillet.
4. Toss in the cubed chicken to cook for about ten minutes.
5. Make the salad in a large salad bowl or divide it into single-serving bowls.
6. Serve with your choice of dressing.

Chickpea Salad

Servings: 4
Total Required Time: 25 minutes

Essential Ingredients:
- Cooked chickpeas (15 oz./430 g)
- Diced Roma tomato (1)
- Diced green medium bell pepper (half of 1)
- Fresh parsley (1 tbsp.)
- Small white onion (1)
- Minced garlic (.5 tsp.)
- Lemon (1 juiced)

Method of Prep:
1. Chop the tomato, green pepper, and onion. Mince the garlic.
2. Combine each of the fixings into a salad bowl and toss well.
3. Place a layer of plastic or foil over the salad. Pop it in the refrigerator to chill for at least 15 minutes.
4. Serve when ready.

Cod Salad

Servings: 4
Total Required Time: 20 minutes

Essential Ingredients:
- Drained capers (1 tbsp.)
- Chopped tarragon (1 tbsp.)
- Mustard (2 tbsp.)
- Olive oil (4 tbsp. + 1 tsp.)
- Black pepper (to your liking)
- Sliced red onion (1 small)
- Baby arugula (2 cups)
- Sliced cucumber (1 small)
- Lemon juice (2 tbsp.)
- Boneless & skinless cod (4 medium fillets)

Method of Prep:
1. Whisk the tarragon with oil (2 tbsp.), the mustard, and the capers in a mixing bowl.
2. Warm the pan with oil (1 tsp.) using a medium-high temperature setting.
3. Arrange the fish in the pan with a dusting of black pepper.
4. Set a timer to simmer for about six minutes per side and cut into medium cubes.
5. Prepare the salad by combining the arugula, onion, lemon juice, cucumber, and cod. Add the mustard mix and toss well before serving.

Combo Bean Salad

Servings: 4
Total Required Time: 8 minutes + 2 hours to chill

Essential Ingredients:
- Tomato (1 medium)
- Red onion (.25 cup)
- Fresh parsley (.5 cup)
- Garbanzo beans (15.5 oz./440 g)
- Kidney beans (15 oz./430 g)
- Lemon (1 - juiced and zested)
- Salt (.5 tsp.)
- Capers (1 tsp.)
- Olive oil (3 tbsp.)

Method of Prep:
1. Chop the tomato, onion, and parsley. Rinse and drain the capers and both types of beans.
2. Toss each of the fixings in a big mixing bowl.
3. Cover with a top or layer of foil. Pop it into the fridge for about two hours.
4. Stir occasionally to mix the flavors before serving

Fennel - Citrus & Avocado Salad

Servings: 4-6
Total Required Time: 35 minutes

Essential Ingredients:
- Lemon juice (1 lemon)
- Fennel - fronds reserved - optional - (1 bulb)
- Avocados (2)
- Fresh parsley (2 tbsp.)
- Olive oil (3 tbsp.)
- Kosher salt (1 tsp.)
- Black pepper (.5 tsp.)
- Arugula (6 cups)
- Oranges (2)
- Blood oranges (2)
- Ruby-red grapefruit (1)
- Fresh mint (1 tbsp.)

Method of Prep:

1. Quarter and thinly slice the fennel. Pit, chop the avocados into halves, and thinly slice them.
2. Finely chop the mint and parsley. Mix the oil with freshly juiced lemon, mint, salt, parsley, and pepper to combine.
3. Combine the arugula and the dressing. Portion the salad into each serving plate.
4. Peel and chop the oranges and grapefruit.
5. Set up the salad fixings finishing with four to five avocado slices to serve.

Feta Tomato Salad

Servings: 4
Total Required Time: 6 minutes

Essential Ingredients:
- Cherry/grape tomatoes (1 lb./450 g)
- Sweet onion (.5 cup)
- Balsamic vinegar (2 tbsp.)
- Salt (.5 tsp.)
- Crumbled feta cheese (.25 cup)
- Freshly minced basil (1.5 tsp.) or dried (.5 tsp.)
- Olive oil (2 tbsp.)

Method of Prep:
1. Measure each of the fixings before you begin.
2. Whisk the vinegar with salt and basil.
3. Coarsely chop and toss the onion into the vinegar mixture. Let it rest for about five minutes.
4. Slice the tomatoes into halves and stir in with the feta cheese and oil evenly to serve.

Healthy Detox Salad with Lemon-Parsley Dressing

Servings: 2 large
Total Required Time: 25 minutes

Essential Ingredients:

The Dressing:
- Avocado oil (1/3 cup)
- Fresh parsley (.5 cup)
- Stone-ground mustard (2 tsp.)
- Pure maple syrup (2 tsp.)
- Lemon juice - fresh (1/3 cup)
- Sea salt (as desired to taste)

The Salad:
- Raw almonds (.5 cup)
- Baby kale (2 cups)
- Carrots (2)
- Red cabbage (2 cups)
- Broccoli (2 cups - florets)
- Bell pepper (half of 1 red)
- Radishes (3)
- Green onion (4 stalks)
- Large avocado (1)

Method of Prep:
1. Measure and add the dressing fixings into a blender - mix until well-combined. Set aside for now.
2. Set the oven to 375° Fahrenheit/191° Celsius.
3. Spread the almonds on a cookie tray. Roast them for five minutes, until golden brown. Scoop them onto a cutting board and chop once cool enough to handle.
4. Prep the veggies. Peel and grate the carrot. Slice the pepper into matchsticks. Thinly slice the cabbage and radishes, and chop the florets and green onion. Dice the avocado.

5. Add the ingredients for the salad to a big mixing container. Drizzle a bit of dressing over the salad - tossing till it's covered.
6. Serve immediately as an entree in bowls!

Vinaigrette Vegetable Salad

Servings: 6
Total Required Time: 10 minutes

Essential Ingredients:
- Cucumber (1 medium)
- Cherry tomatoes (1 cup)
- Red onion (.25 cup)
- Green or colored bell pepper (1 medium)
- Salt (.25 tsp.)
- Celery seed (.25 tsp.)
- White vinegar or seasoned vinegar (1 tbsp.)
- Olive oil (2 tbsp.)

Method of Prep:
1. Slice the pepper into one-inch strips. Slice the tomatoes into halves. Slice the cucumber and dice the onion.
2. Combine the cucumber with the pepper, tomatoes, and onion in a mixing container.
3. Sprinkle it with salt and celery seed.
4. Whisk the oil and vinegar in another container and drizzle it over the salad and toss to coat.

Veggie Meal Dishes

Mediterranean Quinoa & Chickpea Bowl

Servings: 4
Total Required Time: 20-25 minutes

Essential Ingredients:
- Roasted red peppers (200 g/7 oz. jar.)
- Slivered almonds (.25 cup)
- Olive oil (4 tbsp. - divided)
- Garlic clove (1 small)
- Paprika (1 tsp.)
- Optional: Crushed red pepper (.25 tsp.)
- Ground cumin (.5 tsp.)
- Quinoa - cooked (2 cups)
- Kalamata olives (.25 cup)
- Red onion (.25 cup)
- Chickpeas (430 g/15 oz. can)
- Cucumber (1 cup)
- Crumbled feta cheese (.25 cup)
- Fresh parsley (2 tbsp.)

Method of Prep:
1. Rinse the red peppers and mince the garlic. Finely chop the parsley.
2. Chop the olives, red onion, and cucumber.
3. Dump the beans into a colander to rinse thoroughly.
4. Place peppers, almonds, oil (2 tbsp.), paprika, garlic, cumin, and crushed red pepper in a food processor.
5. Pulse till it's incorporated and smooth.
6. Combine the quinoa with the onions, olives, and the rest of the oil (2 tbsp.) in a medium mixing container.
7. Portion the quinoa mixture into four bowls and top with equal amounts of cucumber, chickpeas, and pepper sauce. Garnish using a bit of feta and parsley.

8. Meal Prep Tip: Put a lid on each of the bowls and put the sauce into an individual small container to add at serving time.

Roasted Chickpea & Sweet Potato Pitas

Servings: 6 portions or two pita halves
Total Required Time: 30-35 minutes

Essential Ingredients:
- Lemon juice (1 tbsp.)
- Sweet potatoes (2 medium/about 1.25 lb./570 g)
- Chickpeas/garbanzo beans (2 cans @ 15 oz./430 g each)
- Red onion (1 medium)
- Canola oil - divided (3 tbsp.)
- Garlic cloves (2)
- Greek yogurt - plain (1 cup)
- Arugula or baby spinach (2 cups)
- Whole-wheat pita pocket halves - warmed (12)
- Ground cumin (1 tsp.)
- Minced fresh cilantro (.25 cup)
- Garam masala (2 tsp.)
- Salt - divided (.5 tsp.)
- Suggested Pan Size: 15x10x1-inch/38x25x3-cm

Method of Prep:
1. Warm the oven to reach 400° Fahrenheit or 204° Celsius.
2. Peel and cube the potatoes. Add them into a big microwave-safe container. Microwave them covered, using the high setting for five minutes.
3. Rinse and drain the beans. Chop the onion.
4. Stir in chickpeas and onions - toss with oil (2 tbsp.), garam masala, and salt (.25 tsp.).
5. Spread it into the pan. Roast until potatoes are tender (15 min.). Cool slightly.
6. Mince and add the garlic and remaining oil in a microwave-safe bowl. Prepare it using the high setting until the garlic is lightly browned (1-1.5 min.). Stir in yogurt, lemon juice, cumin, and the rest of the salt.

7. Toss potato mixture with arugula. Spoon into pitas; top with sauce and cilantro.

Roasted Garlic Squash with Sun-Dried Tomatoes

Servings: 2
Total Required Time: 1 hour 20 minutes

Essential Ingredients:
- Roasted spaghetti squash (1 medium)
- Kale (1 small head)
- Olive oil (2 tbsp.)
- Sun-dried tomatoes (.33 or 1/3 cup)
- Garlic (1 bulb)
- Walnuts - raw (.33 cup)
- Sea salt (.5 tsp./as desired)

Method of Prep:
1. Roast the spaghetti squash with garlic.
2. Roast the garlic by slicing the bulb's top to remove, spritz it using a bit of oil - wrap it in foil. Put it into the oven with the squash for the duration of roasting.
3. Roast the walnuts if desired (5 min.).
4. After everything has finished roasting and is cool to handle - use a fork to remove the strands of spaghetti squash and place them in a big mixing container.
5. Peel the garlic cloves and smash - transfer them to the bowl with the squash.
6. Warm oil in a big skillet using a medium-temperature setting.
7. Chop and add the kale.
8. Put a lid on the pan and simmer till the kale is wilted (3-4 min.).
9. Drain and add the tomatoes, roasted garlic, squash, and nuts.
10. Simmer - stirring until heated and thoroughly mixed.
11. Add sea salt to your liking with a couple of drizzles of fresh lemon juice. Serve.

Sweet Potato & Black Bean Rice Bowls

Servings: 4
Total Required Time: 30-35 minutes

Essential Ingredients:
- Water (1.5 cups)
- Uncooked long grain rice (.75 cup)
- Garlic salt (.25 tsp.)
- Olive oil (3 tbsp. - divided
- Sweet potato (1 large)
- Red onion (1 medium)
- Fresh kale (4 cups)
- Black beans (15 oz./430 g can)
- Sweet chili sauce (2 tbsp./as desired)
- Optional: Lime wedges
- Optional: Garnish: More chili sauce/ sub with Roasted Red Pepper Sauce (see recipe)

Method of Prep:
1. Toss the garlic salt with the rice and water in a big cooking pot or saucepan - wait for it to boil.
2. Lower the temperature setting and simmer with a lid on the pot till the water is absorbed. The rice should be tender (15-20 min.).
3. Transfer the pan from the burner and wait for about five minutes.
4. Peel and dice the potato.
5. Meanwhile, warm oil (2 tbsp.) in a skillet using the med-high temperature setting and sauté the sweet potato (8 min.).
6. Finely chop and add the onion.
7. Cook till the potato is tender (4-6 min.).
8. Remove the stems, chop, and add the kale to simmer till tender (3-4 min.).
9. Rinse and drain the beans in a colander. Fold them into the mixture to heat.

10. Gently stir in chili sauce (2 tbsp.) and rest of the oil into rice - add to the potato mixture.
11. Serve with lime wedges and another portion of the chili sauce.

Chapter 5: Lunch & Dinnertime Soup Favorites

Anti-Inflammatory Green Soup

Servings: 6
Total Required Time: 10 minutes

Essential Ingredients:
- Spinach leaves (2 cups)
- Diced avocado (1)
- Diced English cucumber (.5 cup)
- Gluten-free vegetable broth (.25 cup)
- Black pepper and salt (as desired)

Method of Prep:
1. Toss the ingredients into a blender - mixing till it's incorporated.
2. Add the fresh herbs and serve the soup.

Asparagus - Creamy-Style Soup

Servings: 2
Total Required Time: 20-25 minutes

Essential Ingredients:
- Asparagus with juices (430 g/15 oz. can)
- Chicken broth (1.5 cups)
- Onion powder (.5 tsp.)
- Marjoram (.25 tsp.)
- Black pepper (.25 tsp.)
- Garlic powder (.25 tsp.)
- Heavy cream (.25 cup)
- Salt (as desired)
- Fresh parsley (1 tbsp.)
- Suggested: Immersion blender

Method of Prep:
1. Remove the asparagus from the can. Add enough broth to fill the asparagus can.
2. Roughly chop the asparagus and add the juices into a medium pot - puree them using the blender till the mixture is creamy.
3. Stir in the seasonings and reduce the temperature setting.
4. Add the parsley and salt - simmer until it's piping hot to serve.

Broccoli Soup

Servings: 4-5
Total Required Time: 1 hour 15 minutes

Essential Ingredients:
- Yellow onion (1)
- Broccoli florets (2 lb./910 g)
- Olive oil (1 tbsp.)
- Black pepper (as desired)
- Celery (1 cup)
- Chicken stock - l.s. (3.5 cups)
- Carrots (2)
- Cilantro (1 tbsp.)

Method of Prep:
1. Chop the onion, celery, carrots, and cilantro.
2. Warm a pot with the oil using a medium-temperature setting.
3. Toss in the onions, celery, pepper, and carrots. Stir and simmer (5 min.).
4. Pour in the stock and broccoli. Simmer it using a medium heat setting for one hour.
5. When ready, pulse using an immersion blender. Shake in the cilantro and stir.
6. Portion the soup into two bowls and serve.

Cabbage Soup

Servings: 6
Total Required Time: 50 minutes

Essential Ingredients:
- Olive oil (2 tbsp.)
- Fennel (1 cup)
- Garlic (2 tsp.)
- Carrots (1 cup)
- Onion (.5 cup)
- Salt (.5 tsp.)
- Low-sodium vegetable broth (6 cups)
- No-salt-added diced tomatoes (15 oz./430 g can)
- Small head green cabbage (1.5 lb./680 g)
- Ground coriander (.5 tsp.)
- Unsalted cannellini beans (15 oz./430 g can)
- Sugar/or substitute (2 tsp.)
- Fresh oregano (1 tsp.)
- To Garnish: Lemon zest

Method of Prep:
1. Warm the oil in a heavy-duty soup pot using the med-high temperature setting. Chop and add the carrots, onion, and fennel (saving the fronds for the garnish). Cook them until slightly softened (5 min.).
2. Mince and add the garlic, coriander, and salt, stirring (1 min.).
3. Chop the cabbage and oregano. Open the can of beans, rinse them in a colander, and set them aside to drain.
4. Pour in the broth, tomatoes, and cabbage and cook until boiling.
5. Adjust the temperature setting - simmer until the cabbage is tender (20-25 min.).
6. Mix in the oregano, sugar, and beans. Simmer until they're hot (2-3 min.). Serve it with a garnish of fennel fronds, lemon

zest, and enjoy right away for the most flavorful results.
7. Note: Purchase tomatoes with garlic, basil, and oregano included in the can.

Cauliflower Beef Curry

Servings: 4
Total Required Time: 30 minutes

Essential Ingredients:
- Cauliflower florets (1 head)
- Super-lean ground beef (1.5 lb./680 g)
- Olive oil (2 tbsp.)
- Allspice (.25 tsp.)
- Cumin (.5 tsp.)
- Garlic-ginger paste (1 tbsp.)
- Whole tomatoes (6 oz./170 g can)
- Chili pepper & salt (to your liking)
- Water (.25 cup)

Method of Prep:
1. Warm a skillet using the medium-temperature setting to heat the oil.
2. Add the beef to cook for five minutes.
3. Mix in the tomatoes, cauliflower allspice, salt, chili pepper, and cumin. Sauté it for six minutes.
4. Pour in the water and boil for ten minutes.
5. Serve it warm after the liquids have reduced by about half.

Chicken & Sweet Potato Soup

Servings: 6
Total Required Time: 30-35 minutes

Essential Ingredients:
- Olive oil (2 tbsp.)
- Yellow onion (1)
- Garlic (1 clove)
- Sweet potatoes (4)
- Carrots (2)
- Chicken breasts (2)
- Grated ginger (.5 tsp.)
- Black pepper (1 pinch)
- Ground cumin (.5 tsp.)
- Vegetable stock - l.s. (20 oz./570 g)

Method of Prep:
1. Mince the ginger and garlic clove. Chop the onion, carrots, and potatoes. Cube the chicken.
2. Pour the oil into a soup pot and set the burner using the medium-high heat setting.
3. When hot, toss the garlic and onion into the pot. Stir and continue cooking for another five minutes.
4. Fold in the potatoes and carrots. Cook for five more minutes.
5. Fold in the chicken, cumin, ginger, and pepper. Mix in the stock.
6. Adjust the temperature setting and simmer for another ten minutes.
7. Pour into bowls and serve.

Curried-Style Fish Stew

Servings: 6
Total Required Time: 35 minutes

Essential Ingredients:
- Cauliflower (1 head - chopped)
- Chopped onion (1 medium)
- Olive oil (1 tbsp.)
- Garlic (3 cloves)
- Curry powder (2 tbsp.)
- Fish/vegetable broth (2 cups)
- Firm - cubed whitefish – ex. halibut/cod (1.5 lb./680 g)
- Cayenne pepper - ground (1 tsp.)
- Black pepper & salt (as desired)
- Tomato paste (1 tbsp.)
- Coconut milk - full-fat (380 g/13.5 oz. can)

Method of Prep:
1. Use a big pan to warm the oil using a medium-temperature setting.
2. Mince and sauté the garlic and onion for 5 to 7 minutes. Once they're translucent, stir in the cauliflower, curry powder, and tomato paste. Continue sauteing for 10 to 15 minutes.
3. Sprinkle it with salt, pepper, and cayenne. Simmer for one to two minutes more.
4. Mix in the milk and simmer on low until ready to serve.
5. Enjoy the delicious stew for up to four days.

Greek Lentil Soup

Servings: 4
Total Required Time: 1 hour 15-20 minutes

Essential Ingredients:
- Garlic (1 tbsp.)
- Onion (1)
- Large carrot (1)
- Brown lentils (8 oz./230 g)
- Olive oil (.25 cup/as needed)
- Water (1 quart)
- Dried oregano (1 pinch)
- Bay leaves (2)
- Rosemary - dried and crushed (a pinch)
- Tomato paste (1 tbsp.)
- Black pepper & salt (as desired)
- Optional: Vinegar - red wine (1 tsp.)

Method of Prep:
1. Chop the garlic, onion, and carrot.
2. Prep the lentils in a saucepan. Add water to cover them by about one inch. Once the beans start boiling, cook them until tender (10 min.). Empty them into a colander to drain.
3. Warm the oil in a pan using a medium-temperature setting. Toss in the onion, carrot, and garlic. Simmer for approximately five minutes.
4. Pour in the water, lentils, oregano, bay leaves, and rosemary. Once boiling, adjust the temperature setting to a med-low and cover.
5. Cook for an additional ten minutes.
6. Sprinkle it with pepper and salt. Stir in the tomato paste.
7. Place a lid on the pot to simmer for 30-40 minutes. Add water and stir as needed.
8. When ready to serve, drizzle with the vinegar and one teaspoon of olive oil.

Healthy Egg Drop Soup

Servings: 6 @ 2 cups each
Total Required Time: 20-25 minutes

Essential Ingredients:
- Vegetable broth (2 quarts/1.9 L.)
- Freshly chopped ginger (1 tbsp.)
- Turmeric (1 tbsp.)
- Sliced chili pepper (1 small)
- Coconut aminos (2 tbsp.)
- Minced garlic cloves (2)
- Large eggs (4)
- Mushrooms (2 cups)
- Chopped spinach (4 cups)
- Sliced spring onions (2 medium)
- Freshly chopped cilantro (2 tbsp.)
- Black pepper (to your liking)
- Pink Himalayan (1 tsp.)
- For serving: Olive oil (6 tbsp.)

Method of Prep:
1. Prepare the fixings. Grate the ginger root and turmeric. Mince the garlic cloves and slice the peppers and mushrooms.
2. Chop the chard stalks and leaves. Separate the stalks from the leaves. Dump the vegetable stock into a soup pot and simmer until it begins to boil. Toss in the garlic, ginger, turmeric, chard stalks, mushrooms, coconut aminos, and chili peppers. Boil for approximately five minutes.
3. Fold in the chard leaves and simmer for one minute.
4. Whip the eggs in a dish and slowly mix them into the soup. Stir until the egg is done and set it on the counter.
5. Slice the onions and chop the cilantro. Toss them into the pot.
6. Serve the egg drop soup with a sprinkle of oil (1 tbsp. per serving).

Minty Avocado Chilled Soup

Servings: 2
Total Required Time: 15 minutes

Essential Ingredients:
- Romaine lettuce (2 leaves)
- Ripened avocado (1 medium)
- Coconut milk (1 cup)
- Lime juice (1 tbsp.)
- Fresh mint (20 leaves)
- Salt (to your liking)

Method of Prep:
1. Combine all of the fixings into a blender and mix well - thick but not puree-like.
2. Chill in the fridge for five to ten minutes before serving.

Turmeric Chicken Soup

Servings: 3-4
Total Required Time: 45 minutes

Essential Ingredients:
- Avocado oil (1 tbsp.)
- Yellow onion (half of 1 small)
- Carrots (2 large)
- Parsnip (1 large)
- Celery (3 stalks)
- Garlic (3 cloves)
- Chicken breasts (1 lb.)
- Dried parsley (2 tsp.)
- Ground ginger (.5 tsp.)
- Sea salt (.5 tsp./as desired)
- Ground turmeric (1 tsp.)
- Chicken bone broth (3 cups)
- Coconut milk - full fat (.66 or 2/3 cup)
- Kale (1 small head - chopped)

Method of Prep:
1. Warm the oil in an oversized stockpot or Dutch oven using a medium-temperature setting.
2. Mince and sauté the onion, occasionally stir, till they're translucent (5-8 min.).
3. Thoroughly rinse the veggies and prep them. Chop the celery. Peel and chop the parsnips and carrots. Finely dice/mince the garlic.
4. Toss the parsnips, carrots, garlic, and celery; sauté till they are softened, stirring intermittently (al dente 3-5 min.).
5. Trim the chicken - removing all bones and fat. Chop and add it to the pot and cook to brown the meat (2-3 min.).
6. Thoroughly mix in the remainder of the fixings and cover with a lid. Simmer gently for about ½ hour (ideally one hour).
7. Taste test and spices as desired to serve.

White Bean & Chicken Soup

Servings: 6
Total Required Time: 15 minutes

Essential Ingredients:
- Cooked cannellini beans (15 oz./430 g)
- Cooked shredded chicken (4 cups)
- Leeks - ¼-inch rounds (2)
- Fresh sage (1 tbsp.)
- Chicken broth (28 oz./790 g)
- Olive oil (2 tsp.)
- Water (2 cups)

Method of Prep:
1. Pour the oil into a saucepan to warm using the med-high temperature setting.
2. Add the leeks and simmer for three minutes. Chop and mix in the sage and continue cooking ½ of a minute.
3. Pour in the water and chicken broth. Adjust the temperature setting to high and let it boil.
4. Toss in the chicken and put a top on the pan. Stir and cook for three minutes.
5. Serve or save the delicious soup for later.

Chapter 6: Poultry Favorites

Chicken Options

Balsamic Grilled Chicken Breast

Servings: 8
Total Required Time: 55-60 minutes - varies

Essential Ingredients:
- Chicken breast - fresh or frozen (8 @ 110 g/4 oz. each)
- Balsamic vinegar (2 tbsp.)
- Water (1 cup)
- Olive oil (.5 cup)
- Dried onion flakes (4 tsp.)
- Italian seasoning (3 tsp.)
- Ground mustard (3 tsp.)
- Thyme (2 tsp.)
- Black pepper & salt (2 tsp. each)

Method of Prep:
1. Whisk the olive oil with balsamic vinegar, thyme, Italian seasoning, pepper, salt, and onion flakes. Pour it into a one-gallon resealable plastic zipper-type bag.
2. Trim the chicken from all fat and bones. Toss it into the bag.
3. Marinate the chicken for at least ½ hour.
4. Warm the grill. Add the chicken and sear on both sides. Grill it until the meat is white throughout or has an internal temp of 180° Fahrenheit/82° Celsius.

Bruschetta Chicken - Instant Pot

Servings: 4
Total Required Time: 50-55 minutes

Essential Ingredients:
- Olive oil (.33 cup)
- Balsamic vinegar (2 tbsp.)
- Garlic cloves (2 tsp.)
- Black pepper (1 tsp.)
- Fresh basil (2 tbsp.)
- Sea salt (.5 tsp.)
- Tomatoes - sun-dried in olive oil (.5 cup)
- Chicken breasts (910 g/2 lb.)

Method of Prep:
1. Mince the garlic. Remove all of the bones from the chicken and chop them into quarters. Chop the basil.
2. Whisk the oil with the vinegar, garlic, pepper, and salt in a mixing container.
3. Fold in the tomatoes and basil.
4. Put the breasts in a freezer bag with the mixture for ½ hour.
5. Add all of the fixings into the Instant Pot and secure the lid.
6. Select the poultry setting (9 min.).
7. Natural-release the pressure for five minutes, quick-release, and serve.

Chicken with Green Beans

Servings: 3
Total Required Time: 35 minutes

Essential Ingredients:
- Olive oil (2 tbsp.)
- Trimmed green beans (1 cup)
- Chicken breasts (2 whole)
- Cherry tomatoes - halved (8)
- Italian seasoning (1 tbsp.)
- Salt and pepper (1 tsp.)

Method of Prep:
1. Heat a skillet using a medium-temperature setting. Pour in the oil.
2. Sprinkle the chicken with pepper, salt, and Italian seasoning. Arrange in the pan to simmer for ten minutes per side or until well done.
3. Halve the tomatoes. Trim and rinse the green beans.
4. Stir in the tomatoes and beans. Simmer for another five to seven minutes and serve.

Chicken With Yogurt & Mango Sauce

Servings: 4
Total Required Time: 45-50 minutes

Essential Ingredients:
- Chicken breasts (4)
- Plain yogurt (.25 cup)
- Mango (.25 cup)
- Small red onion (1)
- Ground ginger (1 tsp.)
- Black pepper & salt (to your liking)

Method of Prep:
1. Warm the oven to reach 350° Fahrenheit/177° Celsius.
2. Dice the chicken, mango, and onion.
3. Add oil to a skillet and fry the chicken until browned. Toss in the mango and onion. Cook for another three minutes.
4. Stir in the yogurt with a dusting of salt and pepper - adding the mixture to a baking dish.
5. Set a timer and bake it for 25-30 minutes.
6. Serve when ready.

Greek Chicken

Servings: 4-5
Total Required Time: 25 minutes

Essential Ingredients:
- Olive oil (1 tbsp.)
- Cherry tomatoes (1.5 cups)
- Chicken breasts (1 lb.)
- Black pepper (a pinch)
- Garlic (2 minced cloves)
- Dried oregano (1 tsp.)
- Coconut milk (1 cup)
- Lemon zest - grated (1 tsp.)
- Chopped dill (.25 cup)
- Pitted - sliced Kalamata olives (.5 cup)
- Cucumber (1 sliced)
- Lemon juice (1 tbsp.)

Method of Prep:
1. Trim the skin and bones from the chicken. Slice the cherry tomatoes into halves.
2. Warm a skillet with oil using a med-high temperature setting.
3. Add the chicken to the skillet. Simmer for about four minutes per side.
4. Shake the black pepper over the chicken, and add the oregano, garlic, lemon juice, milk, lemon zest, olives, tomatoes, dill, and cucumber.
5. Toss well and cook for about ten minutes.
6. When it is ready, portion it between each plate to serve.

Kung Pao Chicken

Servings: 4
Total Required Time: 20-25 minutes

Essential Ingredients:

The Chicken:
- Coconut oil (1 tbsp.)
- Red bell pepper (1/3 of 1 medium)
- Celery (2 stalks)
- Peanuts (.25 cup)
- Ground ginger (1 tsp.)
- Minced garlic (.5 tsp.)
- Chicken thighs (4 skinless/boneless)
- *Optional:* Xanthan Gum (.25 tsp.)

The Sauce:
- Liquid aminos (.25 cup)
- Sesame oil (1 tsp.)
- Chicken broth (.25 cup)
- Chili garlic sauce/sriracha sauce (1.5 tbsp.)
- Vinegar -ex. - rice wine (1 tsp.)
- Liquid stevia (30 drops)

Method of Prep:
1. Dice the celery stalks and bell pepper into big chunks and set them aside.
2. Warm a skillet using the med-high temperature setting.
3. Chop the thighs into bite-sized chunks.
4. Pour the coconut oil into the hot skillet and toss in the chunks of chicken.
5. Prepare the sauce while the chicken is cooking. Thoroughly whisk each of the sauce fixings in a mixing container - set to the side for now.
6. Once the chicken is almost fully cooked, fold in the veggies.
7. Simmer until they are slightly tender (2-3 min.).

8. Fold in the peanuts - cook for a few minutes while they toast.
9. Add in the ginger and garlic. Stir once more and add in the sauce.
10. Continue cooking and add the xanthan gum to thicken up the sauce even more.
11. Serve with cauliflower rice or on its own.
12. It is also keto-friendly at four net grams of carbs.

One-Pan Chicken Thighs

Servings: 4
Total Required Time: 45 minutes

Essential Ingredients:
- Zucchinis (2)
- Daikon radish (1 cup)
- Sliced carrots (.5 cup)
- Chicken thighs (4 skinless & boneless)
- Olive oil (.25 cup)
- Minced ginger (1-inch cube)
- Balsamic vinegar (2 tbsp.)

Method of Prep:
1. Set the oven temperature to 350° Fahrenheit/177° Celsius.
2. Dab the chicken dry using several paper towels - wrap the skins around the thighs. Place them on a lightly greased baking sheet. Add sliced veggies.
3. Mix the ginger, vinegar, and olive oil. Pour it over the vegetables and thighs. Sprinkle it with pepper and salt. Bake for 30 minutes.

Rotisserie Chicken & Cabbage Shreds

Servings: 2
Total Required Time: 6-7 minutes

Essential Ingredients:
- Precooked rotisserie chicken (1 lb./450 g)
- Red onion (half of 1)
- Fresh green cabbage (7 oz./200 g)
- Mayo - see recipe in sauce chapter (.5 cup)
- Olive oil (1 tbsp.)

Method of Prep:
1. Use a sharp kitchen knife to shred the cabbage and slice the onion into thin slices.
2. Put the chicken on a platter, add the mayo, and a drizzle of oil.
3. Dust using salt and pepper if using. Serve.

Southern Fried Chicken

Servings: 7-8 @ 2-3 strips
Total Required Time: 40 minutes

Essential Ingredients:
- Chicken breasts (4)
- Onion salt (1.5 tsp.)
- Cayenne pepper (1.5 tsp.)
- Dried mixed herbs (1.5 tsp.)
- Black pepper and salt (1 tsp. each)
- Garlic powder (1.5 tsp.)
- Almond flour (1 cup)
- Egg (1 large)

Method of Prep:
1. Warm the oven to 350° Fahrenheit/177° Celsius.
2. Slice the chicken into five or six strips for each breast portion. Arrange on a dish.
3. Combine the dry components, omitting the flour, and mix well.
4. Spice the chicken pieces with half of the spice mix.
5. Make the tenders by dunking each of the slices into the egg and then the almond flour.
6. Arrange them on a greased baking tray - bake for 22 minutes - flipping halfway through the process.

Teriyaki – Slow-Cooked

Servings: 6
Total Required Time: 6 hours 10 minutes

Essential Ingredients:
- Red pepper (2)
- Yellow onion (1)
- Garlic cloves (3)
- Reduced-sodium beef broth (.5 cup)
- Coconut aminos (.25 cup)
- Water (.33 cup)
- Knob freshly grated ginger (1-inch/3-cm piece)
- Pepper & salt (as desired)
- Chicken thighs (2 lb./910 g)
- *For the Garnish:* Green onions (4)
- *Optional for Serving:* Lettuce leaves

Method of Prep:
1. Chop the peppers, onions, and garlic.
2. Whisk the water, aminos, and broth – adding it to the cooker.
3. Blend in the rest of the fixings (omitting the lettuce and green onions).
4. Cook for six hours using a high-temperature setting.
5. When done, garnish with onions, and serve on a bed of lettuce as a delicious taco.

Turkey Options

Black Olive & Feta Turkey Burgers

Servings: 4
Total Required Time: 20 minutes

Essential Ingredients:
- Lean ground turkey (1 lb./450 g)
- Red onion (.25 cup)
- Black olives (.25 cup)
- Garlic cloves (2 - divided)
- Feta cheese - reduced-fat (1.5 oz./42 g)
- Lemon juice (1 tsp.)
- Dried dill - divided (2 tsp.)
- Black pepper (.5 tsp.)
- Salt (.25 tsp.)
- Nonfat plain Greek yogurt (.5 cup)

Method of Prep:
1. Mince/chop the onion, olives, and garlic.
2. Mix the onion, olives, turkey, one clove of garlic, feta (4 tbsp.), dried dill (1 tsp.), salt, and pepper. Make four patties.
3. In another container, combine the feta (2 tbsp.) with the yogurt, salt, pepper, dill (1 tsp.), a garlic clove, and lemon juice.
4. Warm the grill or skillet using the med-high heat setting.
5. Prepare the burgers for five minutes per side.
6. Serve with two tablespoons of the yogurt-feta sauce.

Ground Turkey Bowls with Mushrooms & Cabbage Rice

Keto - Paleo - & Whole30-Friendly
Servings: 3
Total Required Time: 55 minutes

Essential Ingredients:
- Avocado oil (2 tbsp.)
- Yellow onion (1 small)
- Apple (1)
- Garlic (5 cloves)
- Mushrooms (2 cups)
- Ground turkey (1 lb./450 g)
- Zucchini squash (2)
- Ground ginger (1 tsp.)
- Dried oregano (2 tsp.)
- Baby spinach (4 cups)
- Sea salt (1 tsp./ to taste)

The Rice:
- Avocado oil (2 tbsp.)
- Green cabbage, grated (1 large head)
- Sea salt (.5 tsp./to taste)

Method of Prep:
1. Prepare the fixings by dicing the onion, mincing the garlic, and chopping the squash and mushrooms. Peel and core the apple.
2. Warm the oil in a big skillet using a med-high temperature setting. Add the apple and onions.
3. Cook until the onion turns translucent (5 min.). Mix in the mushrooms and sauté for another three minutes.
4. Scoot the vegetables to one side of the skillet - add the ground turkey in the open space. Brown for one to two minutes on one side, then flip and brown for one to two minutes on the other side. Stir the ground turkey in with the vegetables.

5. Mix in the rest of the fixings - stir to incorporate.
6. Put a lid on the pot and simmer till the turkey is thoroughly cooked (5 min.) and the zucchini has softened.
7. Taste mixture for flavor and add sea salt to taste. Serve with cabbage rice (instructions below).
8. Prepare the Cabbage Rice: Chop the cabbage into quarters (or smaller if the head is very large) and place it in a food processor. Pulse until rice-sized shapes form.
9. Warm the avocado oil in a wok or big skillet using a med-high temperature setting.
10. Mix in the cabbage rice and place a lid on the pan. Simmer it, frequently stirring till the cabbage has begun to soften and turn golden-brown (8 min.).

Mediterranean Turkey Skillet

Servings: 6
Total Required Time: 20 minutes

Essential Ingredients:
- Olive oil (1 tbsp.)
- Lean ground turkey (20 oz./570 g pkg.)
- Zucchini (2 medium)
- Medium onion (1)
- Banana peppers (2)
- Garlic (3 cloves)
- Dried oregano (.5 tsp.)
- Black beans (15 oz./430 g can)
- Diced undrained tomatoes (14.5 oz./410 g can)
- Balsamic vinegar (1 tbsp.)
- Salt (.5 tsp.)

Method of Prep:
1. Quarter the zucchini lengthwise and cut it into ½-inch slices. Chop the onions and peppers.
2. Rinse and drain the beans. Mince the garlic cloves.
3. Prepare a skillet using the med-high temperature setting to warm the oil.
4. Add the turkey, onions, peppers, garlic, oregano, and zucchini to cook for 10-12 minutes. Drain it and combine all of the fixings.
5. Serve it when the turkey is done (not pink).

Zucchini & Ground Turkey Skillet

Keto & AIP-Friedly
Servings: 3-4
Total Required Time: 30 minutes

Essential Ingredients:
- Avocado oil (2 tbsp.)
- Ground turkey (1 lb./450 g)
- Medium zucchini squash (1 chopped)
- Ginger - peeled & grated (1-inch nub)
- Green onions (3 chopped)
- Baby spinach (1 handful)
- Coconut aminos (3 to 4 tbsp.)
- Dried oregano & basil (1 tsp. each)
- Sea salt (.25 tsp./as desired)

Method of Prep:
1. Warm the oil in a big skillet using a medium-temperature setting. Once the oil is piping hot, add the turkey. Brown it - keep it a brick form for two to four minutes until it's seared. Flip it over and continue cooking (2-4 min.).
2. Now, break the meat into smaller pieces, add the chopped zucchini, green onion, and ginger.
3. Put a lid on the skillet - cook until the zucchini starts softening (2-3 min.).
4. Mix in the rest of the fixings. Put the top back on the pan and simmer until the spinach wilts (1-2 min.).
5. Mix thoroughly and continue to simmer till most of the liquid has burned off (3-4 min.).
6. Serve it and enjoy it with your favorite side dishes.

Chapter 7: Pork & Lamb Favorites

Cilantro-Lime Pork - Slow-Cooked

Servings: 8 (6.5 cups meat)
Total Required Time: 6 hours 10 minutes

Essential Ingredients:
- Pork tenderloin (2 lb./910 g)
- Water (.5 cup)
- Mild taco seasoning mix (1 oz./28 g envelope)
- Lime juice (2 tbsp.)
- Snipped fresh cilantro (.25 cup)
- Wheat flour tortillas (8 @ 8-10-inches/20-25 cm)
  Desired Toppers - Optional:
- Salsa
- Avocado slices
- Fresh cilantro
- Lime wedges
- Suggested: 3-4-quart slow cooker

Method of Prep:
1. Place pork in the cooker. Pour lime juice and water over the pork with a sprinkle of seasoning.
2. Securely close the lid. Set the timer using the low setting for six to seven hours.
3. Transfer pork to a chopping block. Shred the pork using a couple of forks.
4. Return shredded pork and the cilantro to the cooker and stir to combine with cooking liquid.
5. Serve meat in flour tortillas with desired toppers.

Country-Style Slow-Cooked Ribs

Servings: 8
Total Required Time: Varies - approx. 7 hours

Essential Ingredients:
- Boneless country-style pork ribs (4 lb./1.8 kg.)
- Barbecue sauce (see recipe in sauces - 2 cups)
- Minced garlic (.5 tsp.)
- Arrowroot (2 tbsp.)
- Cold water (.25 cup)
- Suggested: 5-quart slow cooker

Method of Prep:
1. Cut the ribs into serving-size pieces - put them into the cooker and pour barbecue sauce over the tops. Sprinkle with garlic.
2. Securely close the lid - set the setting to low until the meat is tender (6 to 7 hrs.).
3. Remove the ribs and tent them using a sheet of foil to keep warm.

4. Strain cooking liquid into a small saucepan; skim the fat.
5. Combine arrowroot and water until smooth; stir into cooking liquid. Wait for it to boil; cook and stir until thickened (2 min.). Spoon sauce over the ribs to serve.

Garlic Pepper Pork with Warm Garbanzo Salad

Servings: 6
Total Required Time: 6 hours 30 minutes

Essential Ingredients:
- No-salt added - Garbanzo beans or chickpeas (15 oz. can)
- Orange/yellow beets (2 medium - about 3 cups)
- Onion (.75 cup)
- Water (.5 cup)
- Pork loin roast (1.75 to 2 lb. or 790-910 g)
- Garlic (4 cloves)
- Salt (.5 tsp.)
- Paprika & black pepper (1 tsp. each)
- Olive oil (3 tbsp.)
- White balsamic/wine vinegar (.25 cup)
- Fresh oregano (2 tsp. + more to garnish as desired) or Dried - crushed (.5 tsp.)
- Fresh arugula/baby spinach (3 cups)
- Sliced pitted Kalamata or ripe olives (.25 cup)
- Crumbled reduced-fat feta cheese (.5 cup/2 oz.)
- Suggested: 3.5 to 4-quart/3.3 to 3.8 L. slow cooker

Method of Prep:
1. Rinse and drain the beans. Trim, peel, and slice the beets into wedges (½-inch thick). Coarsely chop the onion.
2. Load the cooker with the beans/chickpeas, beets, onion, and water.
3. Trim fat and bone from meat. Using a thin sharp knife, cut ½-inch-deep slits over the roast and insert the garlic slices.
4. Dust the roast using paprika, pepper, and salt. Add roast to the cooker.
5. Securely close the lid and set the timer to low for six hours or on high for three hours.
6. Transfer roast to a cutting board to thinly slice.
7. Whisk the vinegar with oil and oregano.

8. Using a slotted spoon, transfer the bean mixture from the cooker to the bowl with the vinegar mixture.
9. Remove tough stems, add the arugula and olives - toss to combine.
10. Serve sliced pork with the bean salad. Sprinkle with feta cheese and, if desired, freshly clipped oregano.

Pork & Cherry Tomatoes

Servings: 4
Total Required Time: 35 minutes

Essential Ingredients:
- Rutabaga (1 lb./450 g)
- Olive oil (2 tbsp. divided)
- Black pepper and salt (.75 tsp. each - divided)
- Cherry tomatoes (4 cups - halved)
- Pork tenderloin (1.25 lb./570 g)
- Ground coriander (.5 tsp.)
- Dried sage (.5 tsp.)
- Balsamic vinegar (3 tbsp.)

Method of Prep:
1. Warm the oven temperature setting to reach 425° Fahrenheit/218° Celsius.
2. Peel and slice the rutabaga into ½-inch wedges. Slice the pork into one-inch-thick medallions.
3. Toss rutabaga with oil (1 tbsp.) and ¼ teaspoon each of pepper and salt in a big mixing container. Scatter the mixture evenly over a rimmed baking tray.
4. Set a timer and roast for 15 minutes.
5. Combine the tomatoes with the remaining oil (1 tbsp.) and ¼ teaspoon each of the pepper and salt in a mixing container. Mix it with the rutabaga on the baking tray.
6. Season the pork with sage, coriander, and the remainder of the pepper and salt (¼ tsp. each). Scatter it over the vegetables.
7. Roast till the pork is cooked, and the veggies are deliciously tender (10-15 min.).
8. Scoop a portion of the pork to a serving plate. Spritz the vinegar over the vegetables and serve with the pork.

Pork Tenderloin with Apple-Thyme Sweet Potatoes

Servings: 4
Total Required Time: 1 hour
Each portion is 1¼ cups potatoes & 3½ oz. meat:

Essential Ingredients:
- Pork tenderloin - trimmed of fat (1 lb. or 450 g)
- Black pepper (.25 tsp.)
- Kosher salt (.5 tsp.)
- Canola oil (1 tbsp.)
- Sweet potatoes (1 lb.)
- Sweet onions - ex. Vidalia (1 cup)
- Garlic (2 cloves)
- Apple cider (.25 cup)
- Cider vinegar (.25 cup)
- Apples - ex. Granny Smith/Honeycrisp (2 medium-cored and cut into eighths)
- Fresh thyme (2 sprigs)
- Bay leaves (2)
- Suggested: 12-inch/30-cm skillet

Method of Prep:
1. Warm the oven to reach 350° Fahrenheit/177° Celsius.
2. Dust the meat with pepper and salt.
3. Warm the oil in the skillet using a med-high temperature setting.
4. Add meat and cook till it's evenly browned (5 min.). Scoop it into a plate.
5. Peel the potatoes - slicing them into ½-inch pieces - toss them into the skillet. Cook them using the medium temperature setting for two minutes.
6. Mince and toss in the garlic and onions. Sauté them till the onions are tender, occasionally stirring (3-5 min.). Stir in cider and vinegar.

7. Return meat and any juices to the skillet. Add the remaining ingredients.
8. Move the skillet to the heated oven. Roast till the meat's internal temp is 145° Fahrenheit/63° Celsius; turning and basting the meat occasionally (20-25 min.). Remove and discard thyme and bay leaves.
9. Scoop the meat onto a chopping block. Cover using a tent of foil and wait for five minutes. Slice the meat into ¼-inch slices.
10. Serve with potato mixture and, if desired, top with additional thyme.

Quick Mu Shu Pork

Servings: 4
Total Required Time: 20 minutes

Essential Ingredients:
- Vegetable oil (1 tbsp.)
- Pork top loin chops - boneless (12 oz./340 g)
- Fresh button mushrooms (3 cups/8 oz./230 g)
- Green onions (4 or .5 cup)
- Packaged shredded cabbage with carrot or a coleslaw mix (4 cups)
- Soy sauce/or substitute of choice (2 tbsp.)
- **Crushed red pepper (.125 or ⅛ tsp.)**
- Toasted sesame oil (1 tsp.)
- 7-8-inch wheat flour tortillas - warmed (8)
- Hoisin/plum sauce (.25 cup)

Method of Prep:
1. Trim fat from pork and slice it into thin strips. Prepare a large skillet or wok, warm the oil using a medium-high temperature setting.
2. Add the pork to saute until slightly pink in the center (2-3 min.) Transfer it to a holding container for now.
3. Slice the mushrooms and onions - toss them into the heated skillet.
4. Cook for about three minutes or until mushrooms are tender, occasionally stirring (3 min.).
5. Shred and add cabbage/carrot mix. Sauté until the cabbage wilts (1 min.).
6. Toss the pork back into the skillet. Stir in sesame oil, soy sauce, and crushed red pepper. Stir until thoroughly heated.
7. Serve meat mixture with tortillas and hoisin sauce if desired.

Sauerkraut & Pork Shoulder Roast - Slow-Cooked

Servings: 8
Total Required Time: 8 hours 15 minutes

Essential Ingredients:
- Sauerkraut with caraway seeds (14.5 oz./410 g can)
- Pork shoulder/sirloin roast (2.5 lb./1.1 kg.)
- Salt & Ground black pepper (as desired)
- Creamy Dijon-style mustard mayonnaise blend (2 tbsp.)
- Nonalcoholic beer (1 cup)
- Suggested: 3.5 or 4-quart/3.3 to 3.8-L. slow cooker

Method of Prep:
1. Rinse and drain the sauerkraut - add it to the cooker.
2. Trim all of the fat from the meat and remove the bones - slicing the roast to fit into the cooker.
3. Spread mustard over the meat with a dusting of pepper and salt. Arrange the meat over the sauerkraut - pour in the beer.
4. Cover and cook using a low-temperature setting for eight to ten hours or on a high-heat setting for four to five hours.
5. Transfer the pork to a chopping block and wait for it to cool slightly.
6. Slice the meat and serve with the sauerkraut.

Shredded Pork Roast for Sandwiches

Servings: 12 (5 cups of meat)
Total Required Time: 2 hours 45 minutes

Essential Ingredients:
- Boneless pork shoulder roast (3 lb./1.4 kg)
- Garlic (8 cloves)
- Ground coriander (2 tsp.)
- Cayenne pepper (.5 tsp.)
- Ground cumin (2 tsp.)
- Onion powder (1 tsp.)
- Oregano - dried (2 tsp.)
- Black pepper & salt (.5 tsp. each)
- Vegetable oil (2 tbsp.)
- Beef broth (1 cup)
- Burger buns/kaiser rolls (12)
  Optional:
- Shredded cabbage
- BBQ sauce (see recipe in sauces)

Method of Prep:
1. Set the oven to 325° Fahrenheit/163° Celsius.
2. Trim the excess fat from the pork. Mince the garlic and crush the oregano.
3. Whisk the garlic with the coriander, oregano, cumin, onion powder, black pepper, salt, and cayenne pepper. Dust the entire roast using the garlic mixture - gently rubbing it in with your fingers.
4. Warm the oil in a Dutch oven. Add the roast - evenly browning on each side.
5. Dump the broth over the roast. Put a lid on the pot and set the timer to cook till it's tender (2.5-3 hrs.).
6. Transfer the meat from the cooking liquid using a slotted spoon.

7. Remove all of the excess fat from the cooking juices - reserving the liquid.
8. After the meat has cooled to handle - shred it using a couple of forks to pull through meat in opposite directions.
9. Mix in enough cooking juices to moisten - reheat in a saucepan using a medium-temperature setting - stirring frequently.
10. Split and toast the buns to serve. If desired, serve with barbecue sauce and cabbage.

Tender Baby Back Ribs

Servings: 4
Total Required Time: 60 minutes

Essential Ingredients:
- Baby back ribs (1 rack)
- Chili powder (1 tbsp.)
- Black pepper & seasoned salt (1 tsp. each)
- Garlic powder (1 tbsp.)
- Coconut palm sugar (.5 cup)
- Paprika (2 tbsp.)
- Onion powder (1 tsp.)

Method of Prep:
1. Discard the skin off the back of the ribs, or ask your butcher to do so before leaving the store or meat market - removing all fat.
2. Mix all powdered ingredients in a bowl to form a rub.
3. Apply the rub to the ribs and let them stay overnight in the refrigerator.
4. Grill the ribs on indirect heat for about an hour or until the temperature reaches 155° Fahrenheit/68° Celsius.
5. Transfer the ribs from the grill - drizzle barbecue sauce (recipe above) over them.
6. Wrap the ribs individually in aluminum foil and put them into the oven at 225 - 250°Fahrenheit until the meat tenderizes in the oven and comes right off the bone (45 min.).
7. Serve hot with additional barbecue sauce for dipping!

Lamb Favorites

Garlic-Thyme Lamb Chops

Servings: 6
Total Required Time: 15 minutes

Essential Ingredients:
- Lamb chops (6 @ 4 oz./110 g each)
- Whole garlic cloves (4)
- Thyme sprigs (2)
- Ground thyme (1 tsp.)
- Olive oil (3 tbsp.)
- Pepper and salt (1 tsp. each)

Method of Prep:
1. Warm a skillet using the medium-temperature setting. Once it's hot, add the olive oil.
2. Season the chops with spices (pepper, thyme, and salt).
3. Arrange the chops in the skillet along with the garlic and sprigs of thyme.
4. Sauté about three to four minutes on each side and serve.

Lamb with Minty Green Beans - Slow Cooked

Servings: 4
Total Required Time: 6-10 hours

Essential Ingredients:
- Himalayan pink salt (.5 tsp.)
- Freshly cracked black pepper (as desired)
- Lamb leg (1 bone-in)
- Ghee/tallow (2 tbsp.)
- Garlic (4 cloves)
- Trimmed green beans (6 cups)
- Freshly chopped mint (.25 tsp.) or Dried mint (.5 tbsp.)

Method of Prep:
1. Warm the slow cooker using the high-temperature setting.
2. Dry the lamb using a bunch of paper towels. Sprinkle it with pepper and salt.
3. Grease a Dutch oven or similar large pot with ghee/lard.
4. Sear the lamb until golden brown and set aside.
5. Remove and mince the peels from the garlic. Dice the mint.
6. Arrange the seared lamb in the cooker and give it a shake of the garlic and mint.
7. Secure the lid and program the cooker using the low-temperature setting for ten hours or on the high function for six hours.
8. After about four hours, switch the lamb out of the cooker. Toss in the green beans and return the lamb to the pot. Note: You can add ½ cup to one cup of water to the cooker if it gets dried out.
9. Let the flavors mingle for about two more hours - till the lamb is tender and the beans are crispy to serve as desired.

Quick & Easy Lamb Chops

Servings: 6
Total Required Time: 10-15 minutes

Essential Ingredients:
- Lamb chops (6 @ 4 oz./110 g each)
- Whole garlic cloves (4)
- Thyme sprigs (2)
- Ground thyme (1 tsp.)
- Olive oil (3 tbsp.)
- Black pepper & salt (1 tsp. each)

Method of Prep:
1. Warm a skillet using a medium-temperature setting. Once it's hot, add the olive oil.
2. Season the chops with spices (pepper, thyme, and salt).
3. Arrange the chops in the skillet with the garlic and sprigs of thyme.
4. Sauté about three to four minutes on each side and serve.

Saucy Lamb & Asparagus

Servings: 1
Total Required Time: 25-30 minutes

Essential Ingredients:
- Orange juice - unsweetened (1 tsp.)
- Lime juice - unsweetened (1 tsp.)
- Curry powder (1 tsp.)
- Garlic (1 clove)
- Olive oil (1 tbsp.)
- Raw lamb shoulder (2.8 oz./80 g)
- Asparagus - raw (.5 cup)
- Suggested: Shallow oven-proof dish + foil

Method of Prep:
1. Mince and add the garlic with the curry powder, orange juice, and lime juice to make the marinade.
2. Cut a one-inch slice of lamb shoulder to the appropriate serving size for one serving and add it into a small container with the marinade sauce. Pop it into the fridge for two to four hours.
3. Use an eight-inch square piece of foil and place it over the baking dish. Arrange the lamb on the foil and surround it with the asparagus spears. Broil it for six to eight minutes - rotating it once. Remove the asparagus as they are browned.
4. Meanwhile, warm the oil in a saucepan. Pour in the marinade to simmer till the mixture has thickened.
5. Transfer the cooked asparagus and lamb to the pan and turn off the heat. Wait a few minutes and serve.

Chapter 8: Seafood Favorites

Broiled Sea Bass

Servings: 2
Total Required Time: 10 minutes

Essential Ingredients:
- White sea bass fillets (2 @ 4 oz. or 110 g each)
- Garlic (1 tsp. - minced)
- Black pepper (to your liking)
- Herb seasoning blend - salt-free (.25 tsp.)
- Lemon juice (1 tbsp.)

Method of Prep:
1. Preheat - either the oven broiler or grill. Arrange the rack about four inches from the broiler.
2. Spritz a skillet with cooking oil spray.
3. Add the prepared fillets.
4. Sprinkle it with garlic and seasonings. Drizzle with lemon juice.
5. Broil/grill until the fish is flaky and opaque for eight to ten minutes. Serve and enjoy with your favorite side dish.

Creamy Salmon Pasta

Servings: 2
Total Required Time: 10 minutes + overnight chilling

Essential Ingredients:
- Coconut oil (2 tbsp.)
- Zucchini (2)
- Smoked salmon (8 oz./230 g)
- Mayonnaise - see recipe in sauces (.25 cup)

Method of Prep:
1. Use a peeler or spiralizer to make noodle-like strands from the zucchini.
2. Warm the oil over the med-high temperature setting. Once hot, add the salmon. Sauté it for two to three minutes until golden brown.
3. Stir in the noodles and sauté it for another one to two minutes.
4. Store the noodles in the fridge to cool overnight.
5. When it's time to eat, stir in the mayo, portion the pasta between two dishes, and serve.

Crispy Skillet Salmon with Lemon-Caper Dill Sauce

Vegan-Friendly
Servings: 2
Total Required Time: 1 hour 20 minutes

Essential Ingredients:
- Spaghetti squash - roasted (1 medium-sized)
- Kale (1 small head)
- Olive oil (2 tbsp.)
- Sun-dried tomatoes (.33 cup)
- Raw walnuts (.33 or 1/3 cup)
- Garlic (1 bulb)
- Sea salt (.5 tsp./to your liking)

Method of Prep:
1. Roast the spaghetti squash with garlic.
2. Slice the top off the bulb, drizzle using a bit of oil, and wrap in foil. Pop it into the oven with the squash for the duration of the roasting cycle.
3. Roast the walnuts for five minutes if desired. Let them cool enough to handle.
4. Use a fork to remove the spaghetti squash strands - toss them in a big mixing container. Peel and roughly chop the garlic cloves - adding them to the bowl with the spaghetti squash.
5. Heat the oil in a big skillet using a medium temperature setting.
6. Chop and add the kale. Put a lid on the pot and cook until kale has wilted (3-4 min.).
7. Drain and add the tomatoes, roasted garlic, spaghetti squash, and nuts.
8. Simmer till the fixings are thoroughly heated and combined.
9. Add sea salt to your preference, or add a sprinkle of lemon juice over the spaghetti squash for a kick of citrus to serve.

Frozen Italian Fish - Instant Pot

Servings: 4
Total Required Time: 25 minutes

Essential Ingredients:
- Water (.25 cup)
- Whitefish fillets (4 frozen/ex. 2 whole sea bass fillets - halved/3-4 oz. or 85-110 g each)
- Cherry tomatoes (12)
- Black olives (12-14)
- Marinated baby capers (2 tbsp.)
- Roasted sliced red peppers (.33 cup)
- Olive oil (2 tbsp.)
- Salt (.5 tsp.)
  Optional:
- Chili flakes (1 pinch)
- Freshly chopped basil/parsley

Method of Prep:
1. Pour water into the Instant Pot. If the fish is frozen, use ¼ cup. Add the fish and the rest of the fixings. Spritz it with oil, sea salt, and chili flakes.
2. Securely close the lid, set the timer for four minutes using the high-pressure setting.
3. At that time, natural-release the pressure (7-8 min.) and open the lid.
4. Transfer fish to a platter, adding the broth and cooked fixings over the top.
5. Serve with a dusting of basil or parsley.

Garlic Roasted Salmon & Brussels Sprouts

Servings: 6
Total Required Time: 45 minutes

Essential Ingredients:
- Cloves of garlic (14 - divided)
- Olive oil - x-virgin (.25 cup)
- Salt (1 tsp. - divided)
- Fresh oregano (2 tbsp. - divided)
- Black pepper (.75 tsp. - divided)
- Brussels sprouts (6 cups)
- White wine - preferably Chardonnay (.75 cup)
- Wild-caught salmon fillet (2 lb./910 g)
- Lemon wedges

Method of Prep:
1. Warm the oven to 450° Fahrenheit/232° Celsius.
2. Skin the salmon and cut it into six portions.
3. Trim and slice the sprouts - set aside.
4. Finely chop the oregano and mince two garlic cloves.
5. Whisk the fixings in a small mixing container with oil, salt (.5 tsp.), oregano (1 tbsp.), and pepper (.25 tsp.).
6. Slice the rest of the garlic cloves into halves. Toss them with the sprouts and seasoned oil (3 tbsp.) in a big roasting pan.
7. Place them into the heated oven to roast - stirring once (15 min.).
8. Mix wine into the rest of the oil mixture.
9. Transfer the pan to the countertop, stir in the veggies and add the salmon on top.
10. Drizzle it using the wine mixture. Dust it with the rest of the oregano (1 tbsp.) and (.5 tsp. each) of the pepper and salt.
11. Bake until the salmon is just cooked through (10 min.). Serve with lemon wedges.

Greek Roasted Fish & Veggies

Servings: 4
Total Required Time: 55 minutes

Essential Ingredients:
- Fingerling potatoes (1 lb. or 450 g)
- Olive oil (2 tbsp.)
- Garlic cloves (5)
- Black pepper & sea salt (.5 tsp. each)
- Fresh or frozen skinless salmon fillets (4 @ 5 to 6-oz./140-170 g)
- Medium sweet peppers - orange/yellow/red (2)
- Cherry tomatoes (2 cups)
- Fresh parsley (1.5 cups/1 bunch)
- Kalamata olives (.25 cup)
- Fresh oregano (.25 cup) or Dried oregano - crushed (1 tbsp.)
- Lemon (1)
- Suggested: 15x10-inch baking pan

Method of Prep:
1. Warm the oven to 425° Fahrenheit/218° Celsius. Cover a baking tray using a layer of foil.
2. Prep the veggies. Slice the potatoes into halves - lengthwise. Coarsely chop the garlic. Cut the sweet peppers into rings and chop the parsley. Remove the olive pits and halve them. Thaw the salmon if it's frozen.
3. **Arrange the potatoes in a big mixing container with a sprinkle of oil (1 tbsp.), sprinkle with garlic, and salt + black pepper (⅛ tsp. each), tossing to coat. Transfer to the baking pan - cover it using a layer of foil. Roast ½ hour.**
4. Combine the tomatoes, parsley, oregano, sweet peppers, olives, and 1/8 teaspoon of black pepper and salt (in the same container).
5. Drizzle with remaining one tablespoon of oil - tossing to thoroughly cover.

6. Rinse the salmon; pat dry using several paper towels. Sprinkle using the rest of the pepper and salt (¼ tsp. each).
7. Scoop a portion of the pepper mixture over potatoes, topping with the salmon. Roast, uncovered until the salmon easily flakes (10 min.).
8. Zest the lemon. Squeeze juice from lemon over the veggies and salmon. Sprinkle with zest to serve.

Lemon Baked Cod

Servings: 4
Total Required Time: 20-25 minutes

Essential Ingredients:
- Lemon juice (3 tbsp.)
- Fresh parsley (2 tbsp.)
- Melted butter (3 tbsp.)
- Wheat flour (.25 cup)
- Lemon (1 grated rind)
- Paprika (.25 tsp.)
- Lemon-pepper seasoning (.25 tsp.)
- Cod fillets (4 @ 6 oz./170 g each)

Method of Prep:
1. Warm the oven to reach 400° Fahrenheit/204° Celsius.
2. Mince the parsley.
3. Use a shallow dish and combine the melted butter with the juice.
4. In another dish, combine the seasonings and flour.
5. Dip the fish in the juice mixture, then the flour. Shake off any excess.
6. Bake for 12-15 minutes until it's easily flaked using a fork.
7. Combine the lemon peel and parsley. Sprinkle over the fish before serving.

Lemon Garlic Shrimp With Zucchini Pasta

Servings: 4
Total Required Time: 15 minutes

Essential Ingredients:
- Medium zucchini (4)
- Raw shrimp (1.5 lb./about 30/680 g)
- Olive oil (2 tbsp.)
- Garlic cloves (4)
- Butter or ghee (2 tbsp.)
- Lemon (1 for juice & zest)
- Chicken broth (.25 cup)
- Chopped parsley (.25 cup)
- Optional: Red pepper flakes (a pinch)
- Black pepper & salt (as desired)

Method of Prep:
1. Rinse and discard the ends from each zucchini and slice the 'pasta' using a spiralizer.
2. Finely dice the garlic cloves. Peel and devein the shrimp.
3. Warm the oil in a skillet using a med-high temperature setting.
4. Add the shrimp in a flat layer using a dusting of pepper and salt. Sauté for one minute, but *don't stir*.
5. Chop and add the garlic and shrimp. Sauté for another one to two minutes on the second side. Transfer the shrimp onto a platter.
6. Mix in the butter, lemon juice, zest, white wine, and red pepper flakes into the pan. Simmer for two to three minutes.
7. Sprinkle the parsley and fold in the zucchini pasta. Toss for about ½ minute to warm it up. Fold in the shrimp and sauté for about one more minute before serving.

One-Pan Salmon & Mixed Vegetables Specialty

Servings: 6
Total Required Time: 60 minutes

Essential Ingredients:
- Yellow onion (half of 1)
- Garlic (4 cloves)
- Purple yam or sweet potato (1)
- Red bell pepper (1)
- Broccoli (1 crown)
- Carrots (2 large)
- Asparagus (1 bunch)
- Avocado oil (3-4 tbsp.)
- Lemon pepper (2 tsp.)
- Dried parsley (1 tbsp.)
- Ground ginger (2 tsp.)
- Sea salt (2 tsp./ to taste)
- Salmon (2 lb.)

Method of Prep:
1. Set the oven temperature to reach 400° Fahrenheit/204° Celsius.
2. Slice the onion and mince the garlic. Trim the asparagus. Remove the core from the pepper. Chop the rest of the veggies and place them in a big casserole dish.
3. Drizzle them liberally with avocado oil (about three tablespoons).
4. Sprinkle half of the sea salt, lemon pepper, dried parsley, and ground ginger (reserve the remaining half of the seasonings for the salmon). Use your hands to toss everything together until the veggies are well coated in oil and seasonings.
5. Bake on the center rack of the heated oven (25 min.).
6. Thoroughly stir the veggies - continue baking for another ten minutes.

7. Meanwhile, slice the salmon into portion-size fillets (if they aren't already). Coat with avocado oil and sprinkle with sea salt, lemon pepper, dried parsley, and ground ginger.
8. Remove vegetables from the oven after the 35 minutes is up and stir well. Make small wells in the vegetables to make room for the salmon. Put the salmon fillets in the casserole dish with the vegetables and bake until salmon is cooked through and vegetables have reached the desired doneness (20 min.).
9. Serve with any additional sides, such as coconut rice.

Shrimp Scampi

Servings: 2
Total Required Time: 45 minutes

Essential Ingredients:
- Summer squash (2)
- Butter - unsalted (2 tbsp.)
- Chicken broth (.25 cup)
- Lemon juice/white wine (2 tbsp.)
- Red chili flakes (.125 tsp.)
- Deveined shrimp (1 lb./450 g)
- Chopped parsley (2 tbsp.)
- Clove of garlic (1)
- Black pepper and salt (to your liking)

Method of Prep:
1. Slice the squash into noodle shapes using a spiralizer tool. Sprinkle with salt and place on a layer of paper towels to absorb the moisture. Wait for 15 to 30 minutes. Blot the moisture away or lightly wring it out with dry paper towels.
2. Measure out the butter and toss it into a sauté pan using the medium temperature setting. Mince and add the garlic - sauté.
3. Pour in the chicken broth, chili flakes, and lemon juice/wine. Once it's gently boiling, toss in the shrimp. Simmer until the shrimp turns pink and lower the temperature setting to low.
4. Taste the sauce and dust using pepper and salt. Fold in the noodles and parsley. Toss to distribute the shrimp and coat the noodles in sauce. You are ready to serve.

Tuna in Cucumber Cups

Servings: 10
Total Required Time: 10-15 minutes

Essential Ingredients:
- Tuna (6 oz./170 g can)
- Cucumber (1 large - cut into 1-inch thick slices)
- Black pepper (1 tsp.)
- Mayonnaise - see recipe in sauce chapter (.33 or 1/3 cup)
- To Garnish: Fresh dill

Method of Prep:
1. Use a spoon with a small bowl to scoop most of the middle out of the cucumber's slices - leaving just a thin line at the bottom to make the cup.
2. Dab the cucumber using several paper towels to remove excess liquid.
3. Chop the cucumber finely and put it into a bowl with the drained tuna, pepper, and mayonnaise.
4. Thoroughly mix the fixings. Use a small spoon to fill the cucumber cups with this mix.
5. Garnish each of the cups with a sprig of fresh dill and serve.

Tuna Salad With Olives & White Beans - Nicoise-Style

Servings: 4
Total Required Time: 40 minutes - varied

Essential Ingredients:
- Solid tuna - white albacore (12 ounces/340 g can)
- Thinly sliced medium red onion (¼ of 1)
- Green beans (.75 lb./340 g)
- Great Northern beans (16 oz./450 g can)
- Sliced black olives (2.25 oz./63 g)
- Hard-cooked eggs (4 large)
- Dried oregano (1 tsp.)
- Olive oil (6 tbsp.)
- Black pepper and salt (as desired)
- Finely grated lemon zest (.5 tsp.)
- Water (.33 cup)
- Lemon juice (3 tbsp.)

Method of Prep:
1. Drain the can of tuna, Great Northern beans, and black olives.
2. Trim and snap the green beans into halves. Thinly slice the red onion.
3. Cook and peel the eggs until hard-boiled.
4. Pour the water and salt into a skillet and add the beans.
5. Place a top on the pot and set the temperature to the high setting. Wait for it to boil.
6. Once the beans are cooking, set a timer for five minutes. Immediately, drain and add the beans to a cookie sheet with a raised edge on paper towels to cool.
7. Combine the onions with the olives, white beans, and drained tuna. Mix them with the oil, oregano, zest, and lemon juice.
8. Toss the mixture with the salad. Adjust the seasonings to your liking.

9. Portion the tuna-bean salad with the green beans and eggs to serve.

Chapter 9: Side Dishes - Sauces - Dressings & Condiments

Side Dishes

Acorn Squash With Apples

Servings: 2
Total Required Time: 25 minutes

Essential Ingredients:
- Acorn squash (1 small - 6-inches/15-cm - in diameter)
- Real maple syrup/ sub for brown sugar (2 tbsp.)
- Granny Smith apple (1)
- Butter - low-fat (2 tsp.)

Method of Prep:
1. Peel, remove the core, and slice the apple using a sharp paring knife.
2. Toss the apple and maple syrup. Set aside.
3. Poke a few holes in the squash. Pop it into the microwave for five minutes using the high-power setting.
4. Rotate the squash after three minutes.
5. Put it on the chopping block and slice it in half. Trash the seeds and load the emptied squash shell with the apple mixture.
6. Pop the container back into the microwave - continue cooking the apples until they're soft (2 min.).
7. Serve the squash with a portion of margarine.

Baby Spinach Bites

Servings: 3
Total Required Time: 10 minutes

Essential Ingredients:
- Baby spinach (2 cups)
- Olive oil (.5 tbsp.)
- Black pepper (1 pinch
- Garlic powder (.5 tsp.)

Method of Prep:
1. Set the temperature of the oven to reach 350° Fahrenheit/177° Celsius.
2. Prepare a baking tin with a layer of parchment baking paper.
3. Rinse the spinach thoroughly and drain. Arrange it in the lined baking sheet along with a spritz of the oil, garlic powder, and black pepper.
4. When ready, serve as a delicious appetizer or side dish.

Baked Zucchini-Feta Noodles

Servings: 3
Total Required Time: 20-23 minutes

Essential Ingredients:
- Quartered plum tomato (1)
- Spiralized zucchini (2)
- Feta cheese (8 cubes)
- Pepper & salt (1 tsp. each)
- Olive oil (1 tbsp.)

Method of Prep:
1. Lightly grease a roasting pan with a spritz of oil.
2. Set the oven temperature to reach 375° Fahrenheit/191° Celsius.
3. Slice the noodles with a spiralizer and add to the prepared pan with olive oil and tomatoes with a dusting of pepper and salt.
4. Bake them for 10 to 15 minutes.
5. Transfer the pan to a cool spot and add the cheese cubes, tossing to combine. Serve.

Brown Rice Pilaf

Servings: 6 - 1.25 cups each
Total Required Time: 45 minutes

Essential Ingredients:
- Olive oil (1 tbsp.)
- Water (3 cups)
- Brown rice (1 cup)
- Bouillon granules - chicken-flavored - l.s. (1 tsp.)
- Onion (1 small/.5 cup)
- Fresh mushrooms (.5 lb./about 2 cups)
- **Ground nutmeg (.125 or ⅛ tsp.)**
- Asparagus tips - cut in 1-inch pieces (.5 lb./about 2 cups/230 g)
- Finely grated Swiss cheese (2 tbsp.)
- Freshly chopped parsley (.5 cup)

Method of Prep:
1. Warm the oil in a big skillet using a medium-temperature setting.
2. Toss in the rice and sauté it till it starts browning.
3. Chop the onion and thinly slice the mushrooms.
4. Slowly add the onion, mushrooms, water, nutmeg, and bouillon granules.
5. Wait for it to boil and lower the temperature setting, place a top on the pot and let it cook for about ½ hour. Pour in water as needed.
6. Trim the asparagus into one-inch chunks and add the tips to the pot. Cover with top - cook for approximately five minutes.
7. Fold in the grated cheese with a parsley topping and enjoy it promptly for the most flavorful results.

Celery Root

Servings: 6
Total Required Time: 25-30 minutes

Essential Ingredients:
- Celery root (3 cups) or Celeriac (1) - as desired
- Vegetable broth or stock (1 cup)
- Dijon mustard (1 tsp.)
- Sour cream (.25 cup)
- Freshly snipped thyme leaves (2 tsp.)
- Black pepper and salt (.25 tsp. of each)

Method of Prep:
1. Prepare a big saucepan using the high-temperature setting to warm the stock.
2. Peel, dice, and stir in the celery root. Once boiling, adjust the temperature setting to low.
3. Place a top on the pan to simmer, occasionally stirring till the celery root is tender (10-12 min.). Scoop the celery root into a holding container and cover it so it will stay warm.
4. Raise the temperature setting under the saucepan to high. Wait for it to boil. Cook with the lid off until reduced to one tablespoon (5 min.).
5. Transfer the pan to a cool burner.
6. Stir in the pepper, salt, mustard, and sour cream. Add the thyme and celery root to the sauce.
7. Reset the heat to medium and thoroughly heat the fixings. Serve it in a warmed dish.

Creamy Coconut Rice

Servings: 4-6
Total Required Time: 40 minutes

Essential Ingredients:
- Uncooked white jasmine rice (1.5 cups)
- Vegetable broth - l. s. (2.25 cups)
- Olive oil (1 tbsp.)
- Shallot (.25 cup)
- Garlic (2 cloves)
- Baby bok choy (2 cups/approx. 1 bunch)
- Baby spinach (2 cups)
- Ground turmeric (1 tsp.)
- Sea salt (.5 tsp. + more as desired)
- Black pepper (.25 tsp.)
- Coconut milk - full-fat (14 oz./400 g can)
- Green onions (2-3)

Method of Prep:
1. Prepare the rice and mix it in with the vegetable broth in a pot - preparing it per the package instructions. Wait for it to boil. Cover and simmer (15 min.). Transfer the pan from the burner - wait for it to steam (10 min.).
2. Prepare the remainder of the fixings. Finely dice the shallot, green onions, and garlic.
3. Warm a big skillet (high sides) using a medium-temperature setting.
4. Add the oil, adjust the temperature setting to low. Toss in the shallot and garlic. Simmer till the mixture is fragrant (30 seconds.).
5. Roughly chop and mix in bok choy, spinach, and each of the seasonings. Simmer for two minutes, stirring occasionally.
6. Lower the temperature setting and add coconut milk (use the entire can- including the water). Simmer with the veggies for five minutes.

7. Turn off heat, mix in rice, and stir in green onion to serve.

Ginger-Marinated Grilled Portobello Mushrooms

Servings: 4
Total Required Time: 1 hour 25 minutes

Essential Ingredients:
- Balsamic vinegar (.25 cup)
- Pineapple juice (.5 cup)
- Fresh ginger (2 tbsp.)
- Portobello mushrooms (4 large/110 g/about 4 oz. each)
- Fresh basil (1 tbsp.)

Method of Prep:
1. Rinse and remove the mushroom stems. Chop the basil. Peel and mince the ginger.
2. Whisk the balsamic vinegar with ginger and pineapple juice.
3. Arrange the mushrooms in a glass dish (stemless side upward). Drizzle the marinade over the mushrooms and cover with foil or plastic wrap. Marinate them in the fridge - turning them once (1 hr.).
4. Prepare a broiler or grill. Lightly coat the grill rack or broiler pan using a bit of cooking oil spray. Position the cooking rack four to six inches from the heat source.
5. Broil or grill the mushrooms using a medium-temperature setting - frequently flipping till tender (5 min. per side) - baste with marinade as needed.
6. Place them onto a serving platter with a dusting of basil to serve immediately.

Grilled Eggplant & Tomato Pasta

Servings: 4
Total Required Time: 30-35 minutes

Essential Ingredients:
- Plum tomatoes - chopped (1 lb./450 g)
- Olive oil (4 tbsp. divided)
- Freshly clipped oregano (2 tsp.)
- Garlic (1 clove)
- Black pepper & salt (.5 tsp. each)
- Red pepper - crushed (.25 tsp.)
- Eggplant (1.5 lb./680 g)
- Chopped fresh basil (.5 cup)
- Whole-wheat penne (8 oz./230 g)
- Crumbled feta cheese/your choice/optional (.25 cup)

Method of Prep:
1. Put a big saucepan or dutch oven of water on the stovetop to boil. Warm a grill to medium-high.
2. Mince the garlic. Slice the eggplant into ½-inch pieces.
3. Toss tomatoes with three tablespoons of oil, garlic, black pepper, oregano, crushed red pepper, and salt in a big mixing container.
4. Brush the eggplant with the rest of the oil (1 tbsp.).
5. Grill, flipping it once till it's tender and charred in spots, about four minutes per side. Let cool for about ten minutes.
6. Chop into small chunks and mix in with the tomatoes along with basil.
7. Meanwhile, cook pasta per its package instructions. Drain it into a colander.
8. Serve the tomato mixture on the pasta. Sprinkle it with cheese.

Pickled Baby Carrots

Servings: 4
Total Required Time: 15-20 minutes + 8 hours to overnight chill time

Essential Ingredients:
- Fresh baby carrots (1 lb. or 450 g)
- White wine vinegar (.33 or 1/3 cup)
- Maple syrup/ sub for honey - your choice (.25 cup)
- Mustard seed (1 tbsp.)
- Dill weed (1 tbsp.)
- Salt (.5 tsp.)

Method of Prep:
1. Prepare a big saucepan with one inch of water - add carrots.
2. Wait for it to boil. Once boiling, put a lid on the pan, and simmer until crispy-tender (6 min.). Drain.
3. Toss the rest of the fixings into a big mixing container. Stir in carrots. Cover and pop it into the fridge for eight hours or overnight, stirring several times.
4. Serve with a slotted spoon.

Shallots & Brussels Sprouts

Servings: 4
Total Required Time: 25 minutes

Essential Ingredients:
- Olive oil - divided (3 tsp.)
- Shallots (about 3 tbsp./3 sliced thin)
- Lemon zest - finely grated (.25 tsp.)
- Lemon juice - fresh squeezed (1 tbsp.)
- Salt - divided (.25 tsp.)
- Brussels sprouts (1 lb./450 g)
- Vegetable stock/broth - no-salt (.5 cup)
- Black pepper (.25 tsp.)

Method of Prep:
1. Warm a big, nonstick skillet to warm oil (2 tsp.) using the medium temperature setting. Add and sauté the shallots until softened and lightly golden (6 min.)
2. Stir in salt (1/8 tsp.), scoop it into a bowl, and set it to the side for now.
3. Heat the rest of the oil (1 tsp.) using the medium temperature setting.
4. Trim and cut the Brussels sprouts into quarters. Add them to the pan to sauté them for three to four minutes.
5. Add the vegetable stock and wait for it to heat. Simmer with the top off of the pan until the Brussels sprouts are tender or about five to six minutes.
6. Scoop the shallots into the pan, mix in the lemon juice with zest, pepper, and the rest of the salt (1/8 tsp.).
7. Serve immediately for the most flavorful results.

Sauces

Basil Tomato Sauce

Servings: 6
Total Required Time: 15 minutes

Essential Ingredients:
- Canned tomatoes - no salt added (4 @ 15 oz./430 g each)
- Olive oil (2 tbsp.)
- Garlic cloves (3)
- Dried basil (1 tbsp.)

Method of Prep:
1. Crush or chop the tomatoes. Mince the garlic.
2. Warm the oil in a skillet.
3. Toss in the garlic and sauté it until lightly browned or about one minute. Pour in the tomatoes and basil. Sprinkle it with pepper and salt.
4. Cook uncovered for about ten minutes using a medium-temperature setting.
5. Serve the sauce over beans, veggies, or pasta.

BBQ Sauce

Total Required Time: 1 hour 30 minutes (approximate)

Essential Ingredients:
- Tomato sauce (4 cups)
- Apple cider vinegar (.5 cup)
- Dry sherry (.25 cup)
- Mustard (.25 cup)
- Onion powder (1 tbsp.)
- Mustard seed (.5 tbsp.)
- Black pepper (1 tbsp.)
- Fresh garlic (4 cloves)
- Cayenne (1 tsp.)
- Paprika (1 tbsp.)
- Fresh thyme (4 sprigs)
  Optional to Taste:
- Maple syrup/honey
- Salt
- Molasses (1 tbsp.)

Method of Prep:
1. Measure and add each of the fixings in a saucepan, excluding the sherry.
2. Adjust the amounts to personal taste and wait for it to boil.
3. Once boiling, add the sherry (this helps to keep the flavor).
4. Simmer for at least one hour.

Greek Yogurt Mayonnaise

Servings: 12
Total Required Time: 5 minutes

Essential Ingredients:
- Hot sauce (.25 tsp.)
- Yellow mustard (.25 tsp.)
- Apple cider vinegar (1 tbsp.)
- Low-fat or nonfat plain Greek yogurt (6 oz./170 g)
- Salt & black pepper (.25 tsp. each)
- Paprika (.25 tsp.)

Method of Prep:
1. Whisk all of the fixings and mix well.
2. Adjust the seasonings to your liking.

Roasted Red Pepper Sauce - Vegetarian

Servings: 1 to 1.33 cups
Total Required Time: 8 minutes

Essential Ingredients:
- Jarred roasted red peppers (.5 cup)
- Smoked almonds or cashews (.25 cup)
- Plum tomato (1 chopped)
- Red wine vinegar
- Garlic (1 clove)
- Pinch of paprika (1 pinch)
- Crushed red pepper flakes (.25 tsp.)
- Heavy cream or non-dairy unsweetened creamer/milk (1/3 cup)
- Kosher salt - fine grain & black pepper (as desired)

Method of Prep:
1. Add all fixings (omit the cream) into a blender or small bowl of a food processor. Blend at low power to chop nuts, then increase speed to high and blend to create a creamy puree (coulis).
2. Transfer sauce to a small saucepan (low-temperature setting) and mix in the cream. Continue to stir till it's warm, smooth, and combined, 2-4 minutes. Serve as desired.
3. Refrigerate unused roasted red pepper sauce in an airtight container and use it within five to seven days. You can also freeze it for up to three months.

Dips

Homemade Hummus

Servings: 8
Total Required Time: 5-6 minutes

Essential Ingredients:
- Olive oil (.25 to .5 cup)
- Chickpeas or cannellini beans (15 oz./430 g can)
- Kosher salt (2 tsp.)
- Black pepper (.25 tsp.)
- Lemons (2)
- Garlic (4 cloves)
- Sesame seed paste or tahini (.25 cup)

Method of Prep:
1. Zest and juice the lemons. Mince the garlic.
2. Add all of the fixings in the bowl of a food processor to make a creamy paste. Taste and adjust the seasoning if desired.
3. Store any leftovers for up to five days in the fridge.

Mango Salsa

Servings: 4
Total Required Time: 5-7 minutes

Essential Ingredients:
- Red onion (.33 cup)
- Mangoes (2 or approximately 2 cups)
- Cilantro (2 tbsp.)
- Lime (1 juice & zest)
- Red Fresno peppers (3 or .33 of a cup)
- Olive oil (1 tbsp.)

Method of Prep:
1. Dice the mangos and onion. Mince the cilantro and peppers. Zest and juice the lime.
2. Combine everything until it is the desired consistency.
3. Serve into four serving containers or a dip dish.

White Bean Dip

Servings: 8
Total Required Time: 40 minutes

Essential Ingredients:
- Olive oil (2 tbsp.)
- White beans – cannellini (15 oz./430 g can)
- Lemon juice (2 tbsp.)
- Roasted garlic (8 cloves)

Method of Prep:
1. Warm the oven to reach 350° Fahrenheit/177° Celsius.
2. Rinse and drain the beans. Slice the tops off of the cloves of garlic and wrap them in aluminum foil.
3. Roast the garlic for ½ hour.
4. In a blender, pour in the beans, oil, lemon juice, and roasted garlic. Pulse until smooth.

Dressings

Asian Salad Dressing – Vegan-Friendly

Servings: 4-6
Total Required Time: 8 minutes

Essential Ingredients:
- Carrots (3 small)
- Shallots (2)
- Fresh ginger (.25 cup)
- Chickpea miso/your preference (2 tbsp.)
- Rice vinegar (.25 cup)
- Toasted sesame oil (2 tbsp.)
- Raw honey/another favorite (2 tbsp.)
- Macadamia nut oil (.5 cup)
- Water (.25 cup)
- Tamari gluten-free soy sauce (4 tsp.)
- Garlic (2 cloves)
- Lime juice (2 tbsp.)

Method of Prep:
1. Peel and roughly chop the carrots and shallots. Mince/shred the ginger.
2. Place all fixings in a large food processor or high-speed blender.
3. Process until incorporated and smooth.
4. Pop it into the fridge to chill before serving.
5. Serve chilled dressing over soft butter lettuce or as desired.

Creamy Salad Dressing or Sauce

Total Required Time: 40 minutes

Essential Ingredients:
- Raw cashews (.25 cup)
- Chia seeds (1 tbsp.)
- Dairy-free unsweetened cashew milk/your preference (2/3 or 0.66 cup)
- Vinegar - ex. - apple cider (1 tbsp.)
- Agave nectar for vegan/raw honey (1 tbsp.)
- Ground turmeric (.5 tsp.)
- Fresh minced ginger (.5 tsp.)
- Curry powder (.5 to .75 tsp./to taste)
- **Mustard powder (⅛ tsp.)**
- **Salt & black pepper (⅛ tsp. each)**

Method of Prep:
1. Measure and add the chia seeds and cashews into a spice grinder or small food processor and grind into a powder (it may clump).
2. Put the mixture into a blender with about half of the milk. Blend until smooth (30-60 sec.).
3. Add the vinegar, rest of the milk, honey/agave, ginger, turmeric, curry, mustard, pepper, and salt. Pulse the mixture to puree until it's smooth (1 min.). Taste and adjust seasonings to your liking.
4. Chill it for about ½ hour for the maximum thickening - allowing the flavors to meld. Briefly whisk or blend the mixture before adding it to the salad.
5. You can also use it heated to serve with steamed vegetables.

Turmeric Salad Dressing

Servings: 2
Total Required Time: 5 minutes

Essential Ingredients:
- Garlic (4 cloves)
- E. V. olive oil OR cold-pressed Avocado oil (.25 cup + 2 tbsp.)
- Lemon juice (3 tbsp.)
- Raw honey (2 tsp.)
- Turmeric (2 tsp.)
- Dijon mustard (.5 tsp.)
- Hemp seeds (3 tbsp.)
- Black pepper (.125 or 1/8 tsp.)
- Unrefined salt (.25 tsp.)

Method of Prep:
1. Toss the fixings into a mini processor.
2. Pulse them until they are creamy smooth.

Chapter 10: Snack Options

Chicken Filled Lettuce Wrap

Servings: 4
Total Required Time: 25 minutes

Essential Ingredients:
- Shiitake mushrooms (3 chopped)
- Ground chicken thighs (1 lb./450 g)
- Oil (2 tbsp.)
- Fish sauce (.25 cup)
- Water chestnuts (2 minced)
- Diced garlic (3 cloves)
- Iceberg lettuce (4 large leaves)

Method of Prep:
1. Mix the ground chicken, fish sauce, chestnuts, and mushrooms. Set aside for 15 minutes.
2. Warm up the oil in a wok or saucepan. Toss in the garlic. When lightly browned, remove, and add the chicken. Prepare until done.
3. Remove and rinse the leaves of lettuce. Pat them dry and add the chicken to each one. Serve with your choice of dipping sauce.

Chicken Kabobs With Lemon Wedges

Servings: 6-8
Total Required Time: 50-55 minutes

Essential Ingredients:
- Chicken thighs (1.5 lb./680 g)
- Red bell pepper (1 medium)
- Olive oil (2 tbsp.)
- Garlic clove (1)
- Sea salt (.75 tsp.)
- Black pepper (.25 tsp.)
- Dried oregano (1 tsp.)
- Dried basil (.5 tsp.)
- For Serving: Lemon wedges

Method of Prep:
1. Discard the skin and bones from the chicken and slice it into 40 pieces. Slice the peppers into 16 pieces.
2. Mince the garlic and mix with the oregano, basil, bell peppers, oil, and chicken in a bowl with a lid. Marinate for about ½ hour.
3. For wooden skewers - soak them in water for at least ten minutes. Spritz the broiler pan with the oil and warm up the oven broiler. Take the chicken out of the fridge and add the peppers and chicken slices to each of the eight skewers – alternating each one.
4. Broil the chicken five inches from the grill for eight to ten minutes, rotating every two minutes.
5. Serve with a slice of lemon.

Lentil Avocado Tacos

Servings: 6
Total Required Time: 75 minutes

Essential Ingredients:
- Yellow onion (half of 1)
- Canola oil (1 tbsp.)
- Garlic (2-3 cloves)
- Dried lentils (1.5 cups)
- Vegetable or chicken stock - unsalted (3 to 3.5 cups)
- Kosher/sea salt (.5 tsp.)
- Taco seasoning - l.s. (2.5 tbsp.)
- 6-inch tortillas (16 toasted)
- Avocados (2)

Method of Prep:
1. Mince or dice the yellow onion and the cloves. Peel and slice the ripened avocados.
2. Warm the oil in a big skillet using a medium-temperature setting.
3. Toss the onions into the hot pan and sauté until softened (4-5 min.).
4. Mix in the garlic - sauté the mixture for another ½ minute. Fold in the lentils with a sprinkle of salt, and add the top.
5. Simmer for 25 to 35 minutes. Pour in stock as needed.
6. Once the lentils are al dente, stir in the seasoning and simmer for another one to two minutes.
7. Taste test and season as desired.
8. Add the mixture into the tortillas and serve with the avocado slices.
9. The leftovers remain tasty in the refrigerator for up to five days. Reheat in the microwave for one to two minutes or until well heated.

Shrimp Kebabs

Servings: 2
Total Required Time: 25-30 minutes

Essential Ingredients:
- Lemon - (1 - juiced)
- Olive oil (1 tbsp.)
- Garlic (2 tsp.)
- Black pepper (.25 tsp.)
- Fresh rosemary & tarragon (1 tsp. each)
- Kosher salt (.5 tsp.)
- Shrimp (12 pieces)
- Wooden skewers (2 @ 8-inches/20-cm each)

Method of Prep:
1. Heat the grill using a high-temperature setting. Soak the skewers in water for a minimum of ten minutes.
2. Finely mince/chop the tarragon, garlic, and rosemary. Whisk the seasonings, herbs, garlic, olive oil, and lemon juice.
3. Peel and devein the shrimp. Toss the shrimp into the marinade and let it soak in for about five minutes.
4. Skewer the shrimp and place them onto the prepared grill.
5. Cook until the shrimp is thoroughly done (2 min. each side).

Finger Snacks

Roasted Almonds

Servings: 4
Total Required Time: 10 minutes

Essential Ingredients:
- Olive oil (2 tbsp.)
- Blanched almonds (2 cups)
- Paprika (1 tsp.)
- Rosemary (2 tbsp.)
- Salt (1 tsp.)

Method of Prep:
1. Toast the almonds in a pan using the med-high temperature setting.
2. Lower to med-low and stir in the rosemary, paprika, and salt.
3. Continue cooking for about three more minutes before serving.

Roasted Pumpkin Seeds

Servings: 8 @ ¼ cup each
Total Required Time: 1 hour 10-15 minutes

Essential Ingredients:
- Raw pumpkin seeds (2 cups)
- Ghee (1 tsp.)
- Coconut aminos (1 tsp.)
- Garlic salt (1 tsp.)
- Cumin (.25 tsp.)
- Paprika (.5 tsp.)

Method of Prep:
1. Heat the oven to reach 300° Fahrenheit/149° Celsius.
2. Combine the cumin, paprika, garlic salt, coconut aminos, and ghee with the pumpkin seeds.
3. Add the seeds (single-layered) and toss with the ghee/oil.
4. Bake until crispy or for about one hour.

Roasted Radish Chips

Servings: 4
Total Required Time: 25-30 minutes

Essential Ingredients:
- Fresh radishes (16 oz./450 g)
- Melted coconut/olive oil (2 tbsp.)
- Black pepper and sea salt (.5 tsp. of each)

Method of Prep:
1. Warm the oven to reach 400° Fahrenheit/204° Celsius.
2. Use a mandolin to thinly slice the radishes, tossing them in a mixing container with a bit of oil.
3. Layer them onto two baking trays, not overlapping, and dust with the pepper and salt.
4. Bake for 12-15 minutes and serve when ready.

Slow-Roasted Cashews

Servings: 4
Total Required Time: 3 hours 5 minutes + soak time

Essential Ingredients:
- Cinnamon (2 tbsp.)
- Water (1 cup)
- Cashews (1 cup)

Method of Prep:
1. Pour the cashews and water into a container to soak overnight.
2. Drain and allow to dry on a paper towel.
3. Set the oven temperature at 200° Fahrenheit/93° Celsius.
4. Toss the cashews on a baking tray and sprinkle with the cinnamon.
5. Roast for three hours. Cool before serving.

Crackers

Almond Crackers

Servings: 40 @ 10 per portion
Total Required Time: 45 minutes

Essential Ingredients:
- Water (3 tbsp.)
- Almond flour (1 cup)
- Ground flaxseed (1 tbsp.)
- Fine sea salt (.5 tsp.)
- *Optional:* Flaked sea salt

Method of Prep:
1. Warm the oven to reach 350° Fahrenheit/177° Celsius.
2. Mix the dough by combining the first four ingredients. Lay it out on a layer of parchment baking paper - cover it using another piece. Flatten the dough. Press the dough into a 1/8-inch thickness using a rolling pin or your hands. Sprinkle using the flaked sea salt.
3. Use a pizza slicer to make the cuts about ½ to 1-inch sections. Try to use triangular cuts.
4. Arrange on a paper-lined baking tray - set to bake (20-25 min.).
5. Thoroughly cool for storage using an airtight container.

Baked Zucchini Chips

Servings: 8
Total Required Time: 2 hours & 10 minutes (mostly unattended)

Essential Ingredients:
- Zucchini (2 whole medium-sized)
- Oil - olive or avocado (1 tbsp.)
- Salt (.5 tsp.)

Method of Prep:
1. Warm the oven to reach 200° Fahrenheit/93° Celsius.
2. **Slice your zucchini as thin as you can (preferably about ⅛ inch thickness).**
3. Toss the zucchini in the oil until it's evenly coated. Sprinkle on the salt.
4. If you have cookie baking racks, use those. If not, use a baking tray (they won't crisp up quite the same on a baking tray, but they'll still taste great!).
5. Bake the chips for 2 ½ hours, rotating the pans about halfway through. The chips are done when they're just beginning to crisp up.
6. Open the oven door and let them cool this way. Serve.

Goat Cheese Crackers

Servings: 12
Total Required Time: 30 minutes

Essential Ingredients:
- Baking powder (1 tsp.)
- Fresh rosemary (2 tbsp.)
- Butter (4 tbsp.)
- Coconut flour (.5 cup)
- Goat cheese (6 oz./170 g)

Method of Prep:
1. Set the oven temperature to 380° Fahrenheit/194° Celsius.
2. Use a food processor to mix all of the fixings, processing until creamy smooth.
3. Roll the dough out using a rolling pin until it's about ¼ to ½-inches thick.
4. Use a cookie cutter or knife to portion the crackers.
5. Arrange them on a paper-lined pan. Pop them into the oven to bake for 15-20 minutes.

Chapter 11: Dessert Options

Almond-Cinnamon Meringues

Servings: 8
Total Required Time: 3 hours 30 minutes

Essential Ingredients:
- Whole almonds (.5 cup)
- Xylitol (4 tbsp.)
- Egg whites (3 large)
- Pure almond extract (.5 tsp.)
- Cinnamon (.5 tsp.)
- Coconut cream (0.125 or 1/8 tsp.)

Method of Prep:
1. Warm the oven to 200° Fahrenheit/93° Celsius.
2. Cover a baking tray using aluminum foil.
3. Load a food processor to chop the nuts with xylitol until they are finely ground.
4. Prepare a container and use an electric mixer (high speed) to mix the egg whites until soft peaks form.
5. Stir in the coconut cream, almond extract, and cinnamon - beating to create stiff peaks. Gently fold in the nut mixture.
6. Scoop eight evenly spaced mounds onto the prepared baking tray.
7. Make a hole in the middle of each one using the back of the spoon.
8. Bake the meringues on the center oven rack until golden and very dry (1.5 hrs.). Turn off the oven and let the meringues dry in the oven until cool.
9. Carefully peel the meringues off the foil to serve or store.

Ambrosia With Coconut & Toasted Almonds

Servings: 8
Total Required Time: 25-30 minutes

Essential Ingredients:
- Slivered almonds (.5 cup)
- Unsweetened shredded coconut (.5 cup)
- Pineapples (1 small/about 3 cups)
- Oranges (5)
- Red apples (2)
- Banana (1)
- Cream sherry (2 tbsp.)
- The Topping: Fresh mint leaves

Method of Prep:
1. Set the oven temperature to reach 325° Fahrenheit/163° Celsius.
2. Core and dice the apples. Tear the oranges into segments. Cube the pineapple.
3. Prepare the almonds on a baking tin, constantly stirring for about ten minutes or until fragrant and golden. Promptly place on a platter to cool.
4. Next, add the coconut to the pan. Bake for another ten minutes. Take it out of the oven and let it cool.
5. Lastly, slice the banana in half. Slice it crosswise.
6. Combine the rest of the fixings into a dish and toss well.
7. Place the mixture into the serving bowls. Sprinkle with the almonds and coconut.
8. Add the mint before serving.

Applesauce

Servings: 2
Total Required Time: 35 minutes

Essential Ingredients:
- Apples - Granny Smith preferred (1 lb. or 450 g)
- Water (1 cup)
- Lemon juice (1 tbsp.)
- Sugar (.5 cup)

Method of Prep:
1. Remove the peel and core - chop the apples.
2. Fill a large pot of water using just enough to cover the apples.
3. Simmer the apples until softened or for about 20 minutes. Add them to a food processor/blender.
4. Pour in the lemon juice and sugar. Pulse until well combined.
5. Add the mixture back into the soup pot and simmer (4-5 min.).

Apricot-Turmeric & Lemon Sugar-Free Bars

Servings: 16 - varies
Total Required Time: 15 minutes

Essential Ingredients:
- Dried apricots (1.5 cups)
- Steel-cut oats - grain-free (1 cup)
- Chia seeds (1 tbsp.)
- Walnuts (.5 cup)
- Fresh lemon juice (.25 cup)
- Organic lemon zest (2 tsp. - divided into increments of 1 tsp. each)
- Vanilla extract (1 tsp.)
- Black pepper (1 pinch)
- Ground turmeric (1.5 tsp.)
- Soaking water (1 tbsp. - from the apricots)
- For Dusting: Shredded coconut (.25 cup)
  For Variety:
- Crushed walnuts
- Cacao nibs
- Almond slivers
- Chia seeds
- Pumpkin seeds
- Suggested: 8x8-inch baking dish

Method of Prep:
1. Evenly cover the baking dish with parchment baking paper. (You may omit the parchment or cut the bars later.)
2. Soak the dried apricots in hot water for about five to ten minutes.
3. Wait until they are softened and dump them into a colander over a mixing container - *RESERVE* one tablespoon of the water.
4. Load the processor with the apricots with the rest of the fixings - (omitting the reserved water), lemon zest (1 tsp.),

coconut, and any other toppings you may be including. Blend until it reaches a dough-like consistency.
5. Add the extra water (1 tbsp.) if it's too dry.
6. Add the mixture to the prepared pan - pressing it evenly to distribute the dough. Top with coconut, remaining lemon zest (1 tsp.), and any other desired toppings.
7. Pop it into the fridge until it's firm (minimum of 2-3 hrs.). It should be soft and sticky.
8. Keep it fresh in the fridge until you want to eat it.

Baked Goat Cheese With Roasted Pistachios & Blackberries

Servings: 4
Total Required Time: 25 minutes

Essential Ingredients:
- Goat cheese (1.25 lb./570 g)
The Sauce:
- Fresh blackberries (9 oz./260)
- Optional: Erythritol (1 tbsp.)
- Ground cinnamon (1/16 tsp. or one pinch)
The Topping:
- Pistachio nuts (1 oz./28 g)
- Fresh rosemary
- Salt

Method of Prep:
1. Set the oven temperature to 350° Fahrenheit/177° Celsius.
2. Combine the blackberries with cinnamon and sweetener - if using and set aside.
3. Bake the goat cheese in the oven until it gets some color (10-12 min.). Remove and let sit for a few minutes.
4. Roughly chop the pistachios and roast them in a dry skillet - dusting with salt.
5. Top the goat cheese with blackberry, roasted pistachio, and rosemary.

Berry Watermelon Pops

Servings: 8
Total Required Time: 10 minutes + freeze - 4 hours

Essential Ingredients:
- Blueberries (1 cup - divided)
- Watermelon (6 cups)
- Raspberries (1 cup - divided)
- Honey - sub agave nectar for vegan (3 tbsp.)

Method of Prep:
1. Place the watermelon, ½ cup each of blueberries and raspberries with honey in a blender - puree until it's incorporated and creamy smooth.
2. Press the mixture through a fine-mesh strainer into a pitcher or large glass measuring cup to remove pulp and seeds.
3. Fill your ice pop molds ¾ full with liquid. Add the remaining whole blueberries and raspberries to the molds. Insert the sticks and freeze for at least four hours or until frozen.

Black Bean Brownies - Vegan-Friendly

Servings: 12 @ 1.5-inch minis each
Total Required Time: 30 minutes + 8 hours to overnight soaking time

Essential Ingredients:
- Black beans (15.5 oz. or 440 g can)
- Coconut milk (1.5 cups)
- Ground flaxseed (2 tbsp.)
- Water (6 tbsp. - cold)
- Coconut sugar (.5 cup)
- Baking powder (1 tsp.)
- Cacao powder (.33 or 1/3 cup)
- Kosher salt (.25 tsp.)
- Vegan dark chocolate chips (.25 cup + more for sprinkling)

Method of Prep:
1. Drain and thoroughly rinse the beans - combine with coconut milk. Refrigerate for eight hours or overnight.
2. Strain the black beans from milk and rinse. Warm the oven to 350° Fahrenheit/177° Celsius.
3. Mix the flaxseed and cold water in a small cup. Let the mixture rest for ten minutes to gel into a "flax egg."
4. Combine the beans with a flax egg and coconut sugar in a food processor. Pulse till it's silky smooth.
5. Add cacao powder, baking powder, and salt. Pulse until smooth.
6. Add dark chocolate chips and pulse two to three times until the chips have been broken up slightly, but not completely.
7. Transfer brownie mix to brownie molds or a baking dish and tap the sheet tray on the table to flatten the tops of the brownie mix.
8. Sprinkle three to four dark chocolate chips on each brownie.
9. Bake (350°F) for eight to ten minutes, or until the crust is firm, but the insides are still soft.
10. Garnish with sea salt as desired.

Blueberry Crisp

Servings: 4
Total Required Time: 35-40 minutes

Essential Ingredients:
- Oats - old-fashioned type (1 cup)
- Pecans (.25 cup)
- Nutmeg (.25 tsp.)
- Ginger (.5 tsp.)
- Cinnamon (1 tsp.)
- Maple syrup (1 tbsp.)
- Coconut oil (2 tbsp.)
- Frozen blueberries (1 lb. or 3.5 cups)
- Suggested: 8×8 baking dish

Method of Prep:
1. Warm the oven to reach 350° Fahrenheit/177° Celsius. Lightly grease the baking dish.

2. Chop the nuts. Whisk the oats with the spices, pecans, maple syrup, and oil till the mixture is thoroughly incorporated.
3. Dump the frozen berries into the pan. Layer the crumble topping evenly on top of the berries.
4. Bake until the berries have softened and the topping is nicely browned and crispy (½ hour to serve.

Chickpea Brownies

Servings: 9-12
Total Required Time: 40 minutes

Essential Ingredients:
- Almond meal (1 cup)
- Organic garbanzo beans (2 - 15 oz./430 g cans)
- Natural almond butter (.75 cup)
- Unrefined coconut oil (1 tbsp.)
- Organic vanilla (1 tsp.)
- Cinnamon (.5 tsp.)
- Sea salt (.25 tsp.)
- Grade B maple syrup (.33 cup or 1/3 cup)
- Almond milk - unsweetened (.33 or 1/3 cup)
- Baking soda (1 tsp.)
- Also Needed: 6-7-inch pan

Method of Prep:
1. Rinse and drain the beans.
2. Load a powerful blender, add all ingredients, and mix into a well-mixed batter.
3. Pour all of the fixings into a parchment-lined and sprayed brownie pan, bake for 30 minutes at 350° Fahrenheit/177° Celsius.
4. Cool it and serve.

Chilled Kiwi Bars

Servings: 4
Total Required Time: 40-45 minutes

Essential Ingredients:
- Bananas (1.5)
- Grated lemon zest (1 tsp.)
- Kiwi (3)
- Lemon juice (.25 cup)
- Coconut sugar (.33 cup)
- Olive oil (1 cup)

Method of Prep:
1. Peel and chop the bananas and kiwi. Grate the lemon for the zest and juice.
2. Prepare a food processor to mix the bananas with most of the oil, kiwis, lemon juice, lemon zest, and sugar. Thoroughly mix.
3. Use the remainder of the oil to spritz the pan and lightly grease.
4. Scoop and evenly spread the kiwi mixture into the pan.
5. Store in the fridge for about ½ hour before slicing to serve.

Chocolate-Covered Strawberries

Servings: 10
Total Required Time: 6-7 minutes

Essential Ingredients:
- Butter/your preference (1 tbsp.)
- Strawberries (10-12)
- Raw chocolate (1 cup)

Method of Prep:
1. Prepare a saucepan to melt the chocolate with the butter - cool slightly.
2. Slice the berries into halves.
3. Use a toothpick to dip each of the strawberries in the chocolate.
4. Arrange them on a serving dish.
5. When done, place the platter into the freezer to chill for at least 25 minutes.
6. Serve when ready.

Chocolate-Dipped Frozen Bananas

Servings: 9
Total Required Time: 30 minutes + chill time varies

Essential Ingredients:
- Dark chocolate (12 oz.) + coconut oil (1 tbsp.)
- Bananas (3 large)
- Salted pistachios
- Spiced/smoked almonds
- Cocoa nibs
- Popsicle sticks (9)

Method of Prep:
1. Prepare a cookie tray with a layer of parchment baking paper.
2. Melt the chocolate nibs with the coconut oil in a microwave or double boiler. Stir until smooth, glossy, and thoroughly melted.
3. Slice each banana into thirds (9 portions total). Insert a popsicle stick into one end of each banana piece.
4. Dip each banana into the melted chocolate - run off extra chocolate into the bowl.
5. Arrange the prepared bananas on the baking tray.
6. Chop the nuts. Sprinkle the bananas generously with almonds, pistachios, or cocoa nibs. Pop them into the freezer to harden.
7. Once they're frozen, thoroughly wrap them individually or serve as desired.

Chocolate Ganache Macarons

Servings: 20
Total Required Time: 55 minutes

Essential Ingredients:
- Egg whites (3 large)
- Salt (1 pinch)
- Fresh lemon juice (1 tsp.)
- Cocoa powder (.25 cup)
- Almond flour (.5 cup)
- Xylitol - divided (4 tbsp.)
- 100% cocoa baking chocolate (6 oz./170 g)
- Coconut cream (2 tbsp.)

Method of Prep:
1. Warm the oven to reach 250° Fahrenheit/121° Celsius.
2. Prepare a silicone baking mat or baking tray using a sheet of parchment paper.
3. Use a stand mixer with the whip attachment to whip the egg whites with the lemon juice, salt, and xylitol (1 tbsp.) until stiff peaks form.
4. Sift more xylitol (1 tbsp.) with the almond flour and cocoa powder.
5. Mix in with the egg whites and gently fold in until thoroughly combined.
6. Using a piping bag or cut the end of a large zippered plastic bag - fill with the meringue - pipe onto the baking tray to make one-inch rounds.
7. Tap the tops with a slightly wet finger if tips remain.
8. Bake for 35-45 minutes. Transfer the tray to the countertop for them to cool.
9. Once cooled, remove them using a spatula and place them onto a clean sheet of parchment baking paper.
10. Melt the chocolate in the microwave at 30-second intervals.
11. Add coconut cream and the rest of the xylitol (2 tbsp.)
12. Dust it lightly using cocoa powder as to your liking.

Cinnamon Custard

Servings: 6
Total Required Time: 50 minutes

Essential Ingredients:
- Coconut cream (2 cups)
- Cinnamon (.5 tsp.)
- Whole eggs (2 large)
- Xylitol (.5 cup)
- Salt (.125 or 1/8 tsp.)
- Vanilla extract (.5 tsp.)
- Caramel sugar-free syrup (6 tbsp.)
- Egg yolks (2 large)

Method of Prep:
1. Combine cream and cinnamon in a heavy skillet.
2. Warm the mixture using a medium-temperature setting, constantly whisking to thoroughly blend, 'just until' the cream begins to steam. *Don't boil.* Transfer the pan to a cool burner.
3. Warm the oven to reach 300° Fahrenheit/149° Celsius.
4. Whisk eggs with the egg yolks, xylitol, and salt until pale yellow and slightly thickened in a small mixing container.
5. Slowly, mix in the hot cream and whisk in the vanilla extract.
6. Add about ½ cup of the cream mixture into each of six (4 oz.) custard cups - or pour the entire mixture into a two-quart round baking dish.
7. Place the cups or baking dish in a roasting pan. Pour enough boiling water (about 4 cups) into the roasting pan to come halfway up the sides of the cups or baking dish.
8. Bake until the custard is still slightly loose in the center (½ hr.). Transfer them to the countertop - leaving them in the baking dish for another five minutes.
9. Carefully remove cups from the water bath.

10. Serve as desired, topping each serving with one tablespoon of sugar-free caramel syrup.

Coconut Chia Seed & Sweet Potato Pudding

Servings: 4
Total Required Time: 50 minutes

Essential Ingredients:
- Sweet potatoes (4 small)
- Freshly grated ginger (1 tbsp.)
- Filtered water (2 tbsp. + more if needed)
- Full-fat coconut milk/your choice (2 cups)
- Chia seeds (.33 or 1/3 cup)
- Cinnamon (.5 tsp.)
- Ground cloves (.25 tsp.)
- Vanilla extract (1 tsp.)
- Shredded coconut flakes (1 tbsp.)

Method of Prep:
1. Preheat the oven to reach 400° Fahrenheit/204° Celsius.
2. Set a timer to bake the sweet potatoes until soft inside (35-40 min.). Set aside and let cool.
3. Meanwhile, prepare the pudding. Use a container with a tight-fitting lid, such as a mason canning jar.
4. Pour in the coconut milk, vanilla extract, chia seeds, cloves, and cinnamon into the container and attach the lid.
5. Vigorously shake the mixture for one minute to ensure all of the seeds are coated with liquid - via no clumps in your pudding.
6. Pop it into the fridge for an hour - shake at least once in-between times.
7. Once the potatoes are cool to handle, discard the skin, and scoop the potato's flesh into a food processor. Add the grated ginger and water. Blend for several minutes until the mixture is completely smooth. Add more water as required.
8. Layer the chia seed pudding with the sweet potato mixture into four containers.
9. Top with shredded coconut and serve.

Coconut Figs

Servings: 4
Total Required Time: 8-10 minutes

Essential Ingredients:
- Figs (12 halved)
- Coconut butter (2 tbsp.)
- Coconut sugar (.25 cup)
- Toasted - chopped almonds (1 cup)

Method of Prep:
1. Toss the butter into a saucepan using a medium-temperature setting.
2. Stir in the sugar and thoroughly whisk.
3. Fold in the figs and almonds, tossing well.
4. Simmer for five minutes.
5. When ready, divide into small cups and serve cold.

Dark Chocolate Cherry Granola Bars

Servings: 12
Total Required Time: 30 minutes

Essential Ingredients:
- Tart cherries - dried (1 cup)
- Oats - quick-cooking/old-fashioned (2 cups)
- Walnuts (1 cup)
- Flaxseed meal (.25 cup)
- Salt (1 tsp.)
- Eggs (2)
- Pure honey (2/3 cup)
- Dark/regular cocoa powder (.25 cup)
- Organic vanilla (1 tsp.)
- Dark chocolate baking chips - ex. - Ghirardelli chips (.5 cup)
Optional:
- More dried cherries + chocolate chips – to sprinkle the top before baking
- Suggested: 9 x 13-inch/23 x 33 cm. baking pan

Method of Prep:
1. Set the oven setting to reach 350° Fahrenheit/177° Celsius.
2. Spray the baking pan with a spritz of cooking oil spray.
3. Load a food processor to pulse the oats with the cherries, flaxseed meal, walnuts, and salt until finely chopped (sand-type consistency).
4. Whisk the eggs with honey, cocoa powder, and vanilla until smooth in a big mixing container. Add the oats mixture to the mixing container, stirring until evenly coated with the chocolate honey mixture.
5. Add dark chocolate chips to the bowl and stir again. Scoop the mixture into the prepared baking dish and spread it into an even layer.
6. Sprinkle additional tart cherries and chocolate chips on top before baking for 20-25 minutes.

7. Cool the bars thoroughly before slicing.
8. Note: They slice best when chilled in the fridge for three hours or up to overnight. Once ready, wrap individually in plastic wrap and store in the fridge.

Fruity Rice Pudding

Servings: 8
Total Required Time: 1 hour 10 minutes

Essential Ingredients:
- Water (2 cups)
- Brown rice - long-grain (1 cup)
- Evaporated fat-free milk (4 cups)
- Lemon zest (.5 tsp.)
- Brown sugar sub/real maple syrup (.5 cup)
- Vanilla extract (1 tsp.)
- Egg whites (6)
- Chopped dried apricots (.25 cup)
- Raisins (.25 cup)
- Crushed pineapple (.25 cup)

Method of Prep:
1. Set the oven temperature at 325° Fahrenheit/163° Celsius.
2. Coat a baking pan or dish with a spritz of cooking oil spray.
3. Add the rice to a pot of boiling water. Cook for approximately ten minutes. Drain thoroughly using a colander.
4. Stir the brown sugar/another substitute and milk into the saucepan and heat until warmed. Fold in the lemon zest, rice, and vanilla extract.
5. Simmer until thick using the low-temperature setting (½ hr.). Cool.
6. Whisk the egg whites in a small dish and add to the rice mixture.
7. Toss in the apricots, raisins, and pineapples, stirring well until blended.
8. Spoon the mixture into the dish. Bake for approximately 20 minutes.
9. Serve it warm or cold.

Ginger Spice Cookies

Servings: 18 cookies
Total Required Time: 23-25 minutes

Essential Ingredients:
- Palm shortening or butter, if dairy is tolerated (8 tbsp.)
- Eggs (3)
- Coconut sugar - ex. Nutiva (.66 or 2/3cup)
- Organic blackstrap molasses (1 tbsp.)
- Ground turmeric (1 tbsp.)
- Black pepper (1 tbsp.)
- Cinnamon (2 tsp.)
- Ground ginger (1 tbsp.)
- Orange essential oil (5 drops) or Orange extract (.5 tsp.)
- Salt (.5 tsp.)
- Cassava flour (1.5 cups)
- Baking soda (.5 tsp.)

Method of Prep:
1. Set the oven temperature at 350° Fahrenheit/177° Celsius.
2. Line two baking trays using a layer of parchment baking paper.
3. Combine palm shortening/butter with the eggs, molasses, and coconut sugar in the bowl of a stand mixer fitted with the paddle attachment.
4. Mix it until smooth and combined (medium-speed).
5. Add the spices, salt, essential oil/extract, and baking soda. Thoroughly mix.
6. Mix in the flour until the ingredients form a dough.
7. Lay a piece of parchment paper on a flat surface.
8. **Using a rolling pin, roll the dough (¼-inch to ⅜-inch thickness).**
9. Cut it into cookies using a cookie cutter or a ring from a wide-mouth Mason jar (3" across).
10. Bake until browned as desired (13-15 min.).

11. Transfer it immediately to a cooling rack to thoroughly cool before frosting.

Healthy Green Pudding

Servings: 6
Total Required Time: 10 minutes + 2 hours of chill time

Essential Ingredients:
- Green tea powder (2 tbsp.)
- Almond milk (14 oz. or 400 g)
- Coconut cream (14 oz.)
- Coconut sugar (3 tbsp.)
- Gelatin powder (1 tsp.)

Method of Prep:
1. Pour the milk into a saucepan with the green tea powder, coconut cream, gelatin, and sugar. Stir well until it starts to simmer.
2. Set a timer for five minutes.
3. When done, divide into cups and store in the fridge for two hours before serving.

Lemon-Blueberry Cheesecake Bars

Servings: 9-16 - depending on the cut
Total Required Time: varies

Essential Ingredients:
  Shortbread Crust:
- Cashews (.75 cup)
- Pitted dates (6)
- Sea salt (.25 tsp.)
- Cinnamon (.25 tsp.)
- Almond flour (1 cup)
- Maple syrup (2 tbsp.)
- Vanilla extract (1 tsp.)
  Blueberry Jam:
- Fresh blueberries (2 cups)
- Cinnamon (.25 tsp.)
- Arrowroot starch (2 tsp.)
- Maple syrup (.25 cup)
- Lemon juice (2 tbsp.)
- Vanilla extract (1 tsp.)
  The Filling:
- Whole cashews (2 cups)
- Coconut milk/your choice - full-fat (.25 cup)
- Lemon juice (.25 cup)
- Vanilla extract (1 tsp.)
- Coconut oil (2 tbsp.)
- Maple syrup (.33 cup)
- Suggested: 8x8-inch or 20x20 baking pan

Method of Prep:
1. There are a few extra steps, but it is so worth it!
2. Soak two cups of cashews in water overnight for the cheesecake filling.
3. Prepare the blueberries with maple syrup, vanilla extract, and cinnamon (med-high temperature setting).

4. Use a potato masher or wooden spoon to mash the blueberries. Once it's boiling, lower the temperature to simmer - continuously stirring (10-12 min.).
5. After the jam has turned a dark purple (berries popped) - make a slurry by whisking the arrowroot starch with the lemon juice in a small mixing container.
6. Extinguish the heat and empty the slurry mixture into the blueberries. Stir until the blueberries have thickened into a jam-like consistency.
7. Add the crust fixings into a food processor and pulse until a sticky dough forms. Press the dough into the baking tray lined with parchment baking paper. Place the crust in the fridge or freezer while you prepare the filling.
8. Load the high-powered blender/food processor with lemon juice, soaked cashews, coconut oil, maple syrup, coconut milk, and vanilla extract. Blend the filling until creamy and silky smooth.
9. Scoop the filling into a mixing container to add the cooled jam. Gently fold the jam into the filling - adjust its taste as desired.
10. Scoop the prepared filling into the crust. Freeze the bars until completely solid (overnight is suggested).
11. At serving time, transfer the chilled bars from the freezer - placing them on the countertop to slightly soften (10 min.).
12. Slice the bars and serve as desired.

Lemon Sorbet - Ice Cream Maker

Servings: 4 cups/1.5 pints
Total Required Time: 10 minutes + 26 hours chill time

Essential Ingredients:
- Water (2 cups)
- Lemon juice - fresh (1.5 cups/from 8–10 lemons)
- Honey (.5 cup + additional to taste)
- Lemon zest (2 tbsp./approx. 2 lemons)
- Optional: Whipped cream (as desired)
- Suggested: Metal loaf pan

Method of Prep:
1. Place the ice cream maker tub in the freezer several hours before prep time.
2. Prepare a small pot using a medium-temperature setting to mix the water with lemon zest and honey. Warm until the honey is liquified.
3. Transfer the pan from the burner and mix in the lemon juice. Taste test for sweetness - adding honey to your liking.
4. Scoop it into an airtight container, and pop it into the fridge until cold (2 hrs).
5. Scoop the chilled lemon sorbet liquid into the ice cream maker to freeze per the manufacturer's directions.
6. Scoop the frozen sorbet into a freezer-safe container such as a metal loaf pan. Freeze for an additional two hours or until frozen solid.
7. Option 2: You can also pour the lemon mixer into a metal pan and freeze it for two hours. Every 20 minutes or so, scrape with a spoon to get air into it.
8. Scoop and serve.

Mocha Chocolate Cake - Keto-Friendly

Servings: 12
Total Required Time: 35 minutes

Essential Ingredients:
- Sugar-free chocolate chips - semi-sweet (6 oz. or 170 g)
- Unsalted butter cut into chunks (.5 cup + 1 tbsp. for greasing pan)
- Cacao powder (5 tbsp.)
- Almond Flour - ex. Bob's Red Mill (.5 cup + 2 tbsp.)
- Powdered keto-friendly sweetener (.5 cup)
- Granulated keto-friendly sweetener (.25 cup)
- Finely ground coffee (.5 tbsp.)
- Salt (.25 tsp.)
- Full-fat coconut milk or milk of choice (3 tbsp.)
- Vanilla extract (.5 tbsp.)
- Unchilled eggs (5 large)
- For Dusting: Powdered sweetener/cacao powder

Method of Prep:
1. Preheat your oven to 350° Fahrenheit/177° Celsius.
2. Place your cast iron skillet in the oven for 15 minutes to heat up.
3. Roughly chop your chocolate and place it into a microwave-safe bowl. Cook using 20-second increments. Thoroughly mix the chocolate each time it is microwaved until the chocolate starts to melt.
4. When the chocolate is partially melted, mix in half of the butter in chunks - microwave for an additional 15-20 seconds.
5. Stir until the butter is melted and mixed into the chocolate, then add in the remaining chunks of butter and stir until smooth.

6. Use a sifter to sift in the cacao powder to prevent lumps. Stir in the almond flour, sweeteners, coffee, and salt, then slowly mix in the coconut milk and vanilla extract.
7. Separate the eggs. Whisk the egg yolks into the batter and place the egg whites in a clean and dry bowl. Use a clean whisk to whisk the egg whites until they become frothy. Continue whisking until soft peaks form.
8. Working quickly, use a spatula to carefully fold the egg whites into the cake batter until just combined.
9. Remove the cast-iron skillet from the oven and add the last tablespoon of butter. Swirl it around the bottom and sides of the pan until the butter is melted.
10. Empty the cake batter into the pan - smoothing the top using a spatula.
11. Place the pan in the middle or top rack of the oven and bake the cake for 20-22 minutes. Allow the cake to cool slightly before slicing and serving. Top with sifted powdered sweetener or cacao powder if desired.

Are you enjoying the information provided in your new book of guidelines? If so, I'd be really happy if you could leave a short review on Amazon; it means a lot to me! Thank you!

Part 3:
Four-Week Meal Plan

Each of the following meal plans has been prepared with a mixture of suggestions. If you want to switch the meals, it's okay. Please enjoy!

Chapter 12: Week 1 Anti Inflammatory Menu

Breakfast	Lunch	Dinner	Snack or Dessert
Day One: Cantaloupe Smoothie	Black Olive & Feta Turkey Burgers	Quick Mu Shu Pork	Coconut Figs
Day Two: Barley Porridge	Cantaloupe Salad	Crispy Skillet Salmon with Lemon-Caper Dill Sauce	Ginger Spice Cookies
Day Three: Baked Eggs In An Avocado	Healthy Egg Drop Soup	Broiled Sea Bass + Vinaigrette Vegetable Salad	Leftover Ginger Spice Cookies
Day Four: Green Smoothies	Cod Salad Almond Crackers	Balsamic Grilled Chicken Breast + Grilled Eggplant & Tomato Pasta	Fruity Rice Pudding
Day Five:	Chicken & Sweet Potato Soup	Greek Roasted Fish & Veggies	Chickpea Brownies

Huevos Rancheros			
Day Six: Blueberry Hemp Seed Breakfast Oatmeal	Roasted Garlic Squash with Sun-Dried Tomatoes	Tender Baby Back Ribs + Ginger-Marinated Grilled Portobello Mushrooms	Leftover Chickpea Brownies
Day Seven: Eggs with Brussel Sprouts	Greek Lentil Soup	Teriyaki - Slow-Cooked	Apricot-Turmeric & Lemon Sugar-Free Bars

Chapter 13: Week 2 Anti Inflammatory Menu

Breakfast	Lunch	Dinner	Snack or Dessert
Day One: Cherry Coconut Smoothie	Lentil Avocado Tacos	Ground Turkey Bowls with Mushrooms & Cabbage Rice	Leftover Apricot-Turmeric & Lemon Sugar-Free Bars
Day Two: Easy Quinoa	Turmeric Chicken Soup	Lemon Baked Cod + Shallots & Brussels Sprouts	Coconut Chia Seed & Sweet Potato Pudding
Day Three: Eggs with Brussel Sprouts	Brown Rice Salad	One-Pan Salmon & Mixed Vegetables Specialty	Chocolate Dipped Frozen Bananas
Day Four: Spinach & Avocado Smoothie	White Bean & Chicken Soup	Bruschetta Chicken - Instant Pot	Lemon-Blueberry Cheesecake Bars
Day Five: Mackerel & Eggs	Sweet Potato & Black Bean Rice Bowls	Sauerkraut & Pork Shoulder	Leftover Chocolate Dipped Frozen Bananas

			Roast- Slow-Cooked	
Day Six: Flaxseed Porridge	Chicken Salad with Pineapple		Shrimp Kebabs + Creamy Coconut Rice	Leftover Lemon-Blueberry Cheesecake Bars
Day Seven: Kale & Goat Cheese Frittata Cups	Cabbage Soup		Pork Tenderloin with Apple-Thyme Sweet Potatoes	Healthy Green Pudding

Chapter 14: Week 3 Anti Inflammatory Menu

Breakfast	Lunch	Dinner	Snack or Dessert
Day One: Fresh Fruit Smoothie	Roasted Chickpea & Sweet Potato Pitas	Zucchini & Ground Turkey Skillet	Lemon Sorbet
Day Two: Bacon & Egg Breakfast Muffins	Anti-Inflammatory Green Soup	Kung Pao Chicken	Leftover Lemon Sorbet
Day Three: Pineapple Oatmeal	Combo Bean Salad	Garlic Roasted Salmon & Brussels Sprouts	Blueberry Crisp
Day Four: Latte Pumpkin Spice Smoothie	Cauliflower Beef Curry	Chicken with Green Beans	Dark Chocolate Granola Bars
Day Five:	Fennel - Citrus & Avocado Salad	Tuna Salad With Olives &	Almond-Cinnamon Meringues

Coconut & Walnut Porridge		White Beans - Nicoise-Style	
Day Six: Avocado Egg Boats	Chicken Filled Lettuce Wrap	Greek Chicken + Feta Tomato Salad	Chocolate Covered Strawberries
Day Seven: Cocoa-Chia Pudding with Raspberries	Broccoli Soup	Country-Style Slow-Cooked Ribs + Pickled Baby Carrots	Leftover Dark Chocolate Granola Bars

Chapter 15: Week 4 Anti Inflammatory Menu

Breakfast	Lunch	Dinner	Snack or Dessert
Day One: Scrambled Eggs Ginger Carrot & Turmeric Smoothie	Tuna in Cucumber Cups	Mediterranean Turkey Skillet	Applesauce
Day Two: Quinoa Pancakes	Curried-Style Fish Stew	Pork & Cherry Tomatoes	Ambrosia With Coconut & Toasted Almonds
Day Three: Egg White Scramble with Cherry Tomatoes & Spinach	Healthy Detox Salad with Lemon-Parsley Dressing	Southern Fried Chicken + Acorn Squash With Apples	Chilled Kiwi Bars
Day Four: Melon Green Tea Smoothie	Mediterranean Quinoa & Chickpea Bowl	Chicken With Yogurt & Mango Sauce	Cinnamon Custard

Day Five: Oats & Cherries	Chickpea Salad	Frozen Italian Fish - Instant Pot + Celery Root	Black Bean Brownies
Day Six: Breakfast Skillet	Minty Avocado Chilled Soup	Shredded Pork Roast + Brown Rice Pilaf	Berry Watermelon Pops
Day Seven: High-Protein Strawberry Smoothie	Leftover - Shredded Pork Roast for Sandwiches	Cilantro-Lime Pork - Slow-Cooked	Leftover Black Bean Brownies

Conclusion

I hope you have enjoyed each segment of the *Anti Inflammatory Cookbook*. I hope it was informative and provided you with all of the tools you need to achieve your goals with inflammatory issues you may be dealing with daily.

Keep in mind; exercise can also boost your diet plan and benefit you in many ways. The pros have stated that research has proven that a 20-minute exercise could suppress the production of "monocytic cytokines" (a type of immune cell to ward off infections and bacteria.). Start right now, and you will be adding these healthy markers to your lifeline.

- Strengthen your bones and muscles with regular exercise, especially for kids and teens. During the aging process, it can also slow the loss of bone density. So keep in mind, muscle-strengthening activities can help you increase or maintain your muscle mass and strength.

- Improvement of your mental health and mood. During exercise, your body will release chemicals to help you relax, resulting in an improved mood. You will be capable of better dealing with stress and lowering your risk of depression.

- Combining your new diet plan with a bit of exercise, you will be playing an essential role in weight control and the fight to prevent obesity that plagues many individuals. To lose weight, you must use more calories than you eat and drink.

- Reduce your risk of heart diseases as you exercise and improve your circulation to strengthen your heart. Maintaining an exercise plan can lower your triglyceride levels as you lower your blood pressure. The increased blood flow raises your body's oxygen levels to help lower your risk of heart diseases, including high cholesterol, coronary artery disease, and heart attack.

- Help your body manage blood sugar and insulin levels with an exercise plan to lower your blood sugar level to help your insulin work better (if you have diabetes).

- Lower your risk of falls (especially if you're aging) by performing balance and muscle-strengthening activities in addition to moderate-intensity aerobic activity.

- Exercise will allow you to fall asleep quickly and sleep longer.

Overall, increase your chances of living longer. Studies show that physical activity can reduce your risk of dying early from the leading causes of death, like heart disease and some cancers. In addition to the recipes, some simple physical exercises must also be indicated, possibly performed at home by anyone. Now, let's see how to accomplish all of these:

Walking is an excellent way to get your daily exercise. Go for a 20-minute walk or pick up the pace while watching a favorite show!

Start Yoga Exercises: The gentle flowing movements combined with deep-breathing exercises will help reduce your anxiety, lower your blood pressure, and improve depression symptoms. You can do yoga anywhere.

Try Cycling: You can choose to connect with nature or opt to have a stationary bike to ride away from those inflamed muscles; try one of these methods.

1. Go for a five-minute warm-up keeping a low-resistance and easy pace.
2. Cycle for 20 minutes at moderate resistance while picking up the pace.
3. Cool-down using the same five-minute span - taking it back down to a low-resistance and easy pace.

You get it now, choose an activity you enjoy, and get that body moving!

I have organized a few extra tips that might help you get motivated and stay organized as you begin your new meal plan. You already have four weeks set up, so you are ahead of the game.

1. Try using meal prep to prepare your favorite meals when you have extra time. You will have healthier options for those times when your schedule doesn't allow time for cooking.

2. Prepare a grocery list before you head to the market. It will keep you more focused and less likely to stroll down the snack aisles!

3. Choose a variety of healthy fats, wholesome veggies, and fruits. Always have plenty of healthy options in the pantry, fridge, and freezer. Having options will keep you from getting bored, and head to your local pizza parlor.

4. Drink plenty of water. Proper hydration boosts your energy level, brain function, and overall health.

It is essential to speak with your primary care physician or another healthcare worker before making any major changes to your diet plan.

If you enjoyed this book, please let me know your thoughts by leaving a short review on Amazon; thank you!

Other Books By This Author

BOWLS COOKBOOK

LEARN HOW TO PREPARE TASTY AND HEALTY ONE-BOWL MEALS WITH MORE THAN 100 EASY RECIPES.

MARTIN CAMERON

Printed in Great Britain
by Amazon